WAKING UP
IN 5D

"Maureen sees the big picture and is able to distill it into manageable chunks. She loves her audience and sees beyond the immediate, providing a compassionate, workable way to navigate in the new 5D energies that are permeating the planet. Her description of the dimensions and experience clearly establishes that most everyone reading this has probably already 'woken up in 5D' at least once! How will you stay there? Read this book!"

SUSAN SHUMSKY, AUTHOR OF *DIVINE REVELATION*

"Everything Maureen St. Germain describes as typical to those who suddenly or purposefully find their consciousness, their ability to move about and live in the world around them, switched to a fifth-dimensional mind-set matches what the average near-death experiencer—child or adult—goes through. Each step she offers, each meditation, each mindful journey through the intellect, intuition, and the heart of all knowing remodels our life. A true guide, *Waking Up in 5D* opens the door to where, sooner or later, most of us will go."

P. M. H. ATWATER, L.H.D., PIONEERING RESEARCHER IN
THE FIELD OF NEAR-DEATH STUDIES AND AUTHOR OF
A MANUAL FOR DEVELOPING HUMANS

"Maureen provides fabulous information and tools that help the reader tap into and maintain a higher more evolved consciousness. This is a perfect read for anyone who is interested in shifting out of struggle and into peace. Use the tools she presents and you will find your world transformed in a beautiful and powerful way."

ALEYA DAO, AUTHOR OF *SEVEN CUPS OF CONSCIOUSNESS*

"Suppose the very thing we needed most was already present in our deepest being. Our task is to wake up to what we already are and possess, and Maureen J. St. Germain explains how to do it in her timely, high-spirited *Waking Up in 5D*—a book about waking up the life-enhancing powers within us that we need to survive and flourish on our bedeviled planet."

MICHAEL GROSSO, PH.D., AUTHOR OF *THE MAN WHO COULD FLY*

"A remarkably timely book. A masterful weaving together of practical and mystic evidence for the profound shift in consciousness so many of us are currently experiencing. *Waking Up in 5D* is engagingly personal—full of insightful examples and stories drawn from the author's life. The book will be a valuable confirmation for those aware of 5D realities and invaluable for those aspiring to make the shift."

TIMOTHY WYLLIE, AUTHOR OF
CONFESSIONS OF A REBEL ANGEL AND *DOLPHINS, ETs & ANGELS*

"This book is not to only to be read, it is to be experienced. Maureen's radiant brilliance shines through in her evolutionary book *Waking Up in 5D*. The tools, techniques, and teachings that are provided are truly a magnificent contribution to the expansion of consciousness happening in humanity. This book will be a gift and a blessing to all those who read it."

LORI ANN SPAGNA, AUTHOR OF *MANIFESTATION MADE EASY*

"*Waking Up in 5D* contains simple practices. It describes as practically as possible the steps you'll need to overpower a limiting third-dimensional view of our world. I strongly recommend this book to anyone ready to ask real questions that can change the course of a life."

SONDRA SNEED, AUTHOR OF *WHAT TO DO WHEN YOU'RE DEAD*

"*Waking Up in 5D* provides innovative tools to shift out of polarity and into oneness and take a quantum leap into consciousness. Maureen has crafted a beautiful tapestry to access the higher self and enter into multidimensional living."

DANIELLE RAMA HOFFMAN, AUTHOR OF *THE TABLETS OF LIGHT*

"This clear, refreshingly insightful book gives practical guidance about how to shift your thoughts, vibration, and consciousness to a whole new octave and in the process change your life. It is a wonderful reminder of how to live our lives with more flow and more grace. I recommend it highly!"

TRICIA McCANNON, AUTHOR OF *RETURN OF THE DIVINE SOPHIA*

"*Waking Up in 5D* is a thoroughly comprehensive survey concerning Eastern and European alternative consciousness. Maureen's instructions and meditations, which comprise the Higher Self Practice, are demanding and rewarding."

D. S. LLITERAS, AUTHOR OF *SYLLABLES OF RAIN*

"This book will give you a clear understanding of how much our paradigm is changing. Read this book and discover what's happening, what's changing, and what's in store for us in 5D."

MADELINE GERWICK, AUTHOR OF *THE GOOD TIMING GUIDE*

WAKING UP IN 5D

A Practical Guide to
Multidimensional Transformation

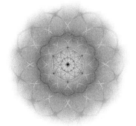

Maureen J. St. Germain

Bear & Company
Rochester, Vermont • Toronto, Canada

Bear & Company
One Park Street
Rochester, Vermont 05767
www.BearandCompanyBooks.com

Text stock is SFI certified

Bear & Company is a division of Inner Traditions International

Library of Congress Cataloging-in-Publication Data

Names: St. Germain, Maureen J., 1951– author.
Title: Waking up in 5D : a practical guide to multidimensional transformation /
  Maureen J. St. Germain.
Description: Rochester, Vermont : Bear & Company, 2017. | Includes
  bibliographical references and index.
Identifiers: LCCN 2017001389 | ISBN 9781591432883 (pbk.) |
  ISBN 9781591432890 (e-book)
Subjects: LCSH: Altered states of consciousness. |
  Consciousness—Miscellanea. | Religion and science. | Parapsychology. |
  Occultism. | Future life—Miscellanea.
Classification: LCC BF1045.A48 S7 2017 | DDC 154.4—dc23
LC record available at https://lccn.loc.gov/2017001389

Printed and bound in the United States by Lake Book Manufacturing, Inc.
The text stock is SFI certified. The Sustainable Forestry Initiative® program
promotes sustainable forest management.

10 9 8 7 6 5

Text design and layout by Debbie Glogover
This book was typeset in Garamond Premier Pro with Versailles LT Std, Gill Sans
MT Pro, ITC Legacy Sans, and Trajan Pro 3 as display fonts

To send correspondence to the author of this book, mail a first-class letter to the
author c/o Inner Traditions • Bear & Company, One Park Street, Rochester, VT
05767, and we will forward the communication, or contact the author directly at
www.MaureenStGermain.com.

This book is dedicated to
the Dragons who have reappeared
on the Earth, to teach all of us about clarity
and help each of us to make the best decisions ever.
My favorite dragon is a human, Devra Jacobs.
She calls herself a dragon, and for sure she is
supportive, helpful, friendly, and
tenacious, just like the unseen
dragons in our world.

Special thanks go to Kelley Knight, Endre Balog, Janiece Jaffe, Terri Young, and Sylvia Chappell and my wonderful students who have inspired me so much.

Contents

Higher Consciousness, Science, and the Heart

Haven't you wondered what you are supposed to be doing on this planet? Haven't you wondered why there is so much difficulty and violence? If you are reading this, you've probably come to the Earth to be part of the solution. Your job is to create Heaven on Earth. This book will help you do that. Becoming part of the solution is a two-step approach. The first phase is to discover a new way to think about yourself and reality. The second phase is to be proactive and choose a new way of being with your evolved understanding.

This book offers you guidance with both of these steps. First, it will deepen your understanding of what lies beyond the third dimension, particularly the fifth dimension, which can best be understood as the place everyone else calls *heaven*. But the fifth dimension is not a place that we are going to; it is instead a vibration we are becoming! So you don't have to leave "here" to get there; you are already where you are. By beginning to notice and understand the differences between 3D and 5D, you will be able to shift more readily into your fifth-dimensional self that is ready and waiting for you! It's far easier than you may have thought! What about 4D? This is a dimension that you will pass through on the way to 5D, as we will see.

This book also offers you the strategies and techniques to use this new understanding. My job is to help you understand what is

1

happening, why it is happening, how we are doing, and how we can be proactive. I am a mystic: I have a permanent guide and am connected directly to Source. All the material I am sharing with you has come to me through my guides.

The fifth-dimensional experience is essential to the future of humanity. It's an emerging notion where science merges with philosophy and spirituality. Our wake-up call is that we are deeply connected to our consciousness, and that our science, nature, and philosophy are becoming merged into a new way of being—*waking up in fifth dimension*. It is the paradigm shift of paradigm shifts.

This book isn't just about *you* waking up in fifth dimension; it's about the universal wake-up call for humanity. It will change the paradigm to our new now. In this book you will learn skills, including the language of fifth dimension, which is nonpejorative and nonpreferential. It is egalitarian yet has tremendous variety.

I have been teaching my students about the dimensions in classes for close to twenty years. I am now ready to share a full explanation of this great dimensional shift. This book will provide you a chance to digest this powerful knowledge along with expanding what is possible for you. Both scientists and mystics agree that there is far more going on dimensionally than we can see or feel with our senses. In fact there is so much more that it merits diving deeper into what the dimensions are and how they are organized. With this understanding you will begin to believe that you have indeed already been beyond the third dimension and will continue to expand your awareness and experiences.

HIGHER SELF CONNECTION
GAME CHANGER

Working with your Higher Self will give you the keys to waking up in 5D. This book will help guide you in that direction. Developing a Higher Self connection is the one key that will unlock everything else. Your Higher Self is different from your lower self that provides intuition yet is tied to your ego/desires. Your lower self is reactive; your Higher Self is proactive. Your Higher Self is ahead of the curve; your lower self is reactive to the curve.

Connecting to your Higher Self is a game changer. A practice to aid you to connect is described in detail in chapter 1. Eventually you will apply this understanding to all you know, and it will greatly expand your loving heart. Your Higher Self will keep you honest. There was many a time when I wanted to do one thing, then chose to check in with my Higher Self, and was given information that helped me choose a different direction, which resulted in my having a more fifth-dimensional experience.

We are collectively being nudged to find a new and different version of ourselves with new and different pathways to solve what is in front of us. In this book, I will teach you what I know, and that knowledge is of the light, yet you do not have to take my word for it. You can and must validate it yourself, by developing your own connection with your Higher Self.

THE HEART LEADS THE WAY

Being in fifth dimension is a frequency choice. It's also about using what's available to assist you when you fall out of the higher frequencies. This means your movement to fifth dimension isn't a direct arrival. Being there doesn't guarantee you'll stay there. Certainly once you've been there it becomes easier and easier to reach. If you do move back into third dimension, it's a movement that will keep oscillating until you can hold the higher frequency all the time.

This is probably one of the hardest concepts to begin to understand. Think about how you might move through a difficult discovery about someone close to you. Maybe you are angry, then hurt, then okay with it, then angry again, and so on. One of the ways to "be in your heart" is to notice these feelings as they move. Then catapult yourself from "being OK" with it to having compassion for the other person, situation, or circumstance. How to do that? One way is the Hawaiian practice of Ho'oponopono (ho-o-pono-pono). Simply put, it is the process of saying over and over, in your thought, "Please forgive me. I am sorry. I love you. Thank you." This system was brought to light and taught by the Hawaiian healer Morrnah Nalamaku Simeona. Joe Vitale popularized it. Try it for yourself the next time you are noticing your hardness of heart is keeping you from moving into compassion.

The heart leads the way. If you have a good mind, use it, and then let your heart decide. This means you should go ahead and let your mind take you through each of the emotions but then keep moving. Don't stop with the negative ones. Your heart leads the way. Nothing else matters!

You get to decide your interpretation of the things that happen to you and around you. I remember a birthday card I purchased for my stepfather. It showed a woman daydreaming at a traffic light, with a lineup of cars behind her. The caption read, "I was thinking about your birthday while I was out driving today, and when the traffic light changed, suddenly all the cars behind me started honking in celebration! Wasn't that nice of them?" It's lovely to perceive that people honking at you are in concert with you or liking you! What a concept!

Imagine thinking positive and supportive thoughts about any bit of feedback you receive. I knew my stepfather would love the card because he doesn't really understand what I do, even though he likes me as a person. He's convinced that whatever it is, it's a nontangible, airy thing to do as my lifework, and he thinks it's even stranger that other people like this "airy" stuff.

I'm inspired by the world I experience, and I have found, over and over, the correlations in the real world to corroborate this understanding. One thing is certain: the future is *not* certain. Although much of our future is assured, how and when it will happen is up to us. It is incumbent upon us to co-create a future that is heart-centered and loving.

CONSCIOUSNESS AND SCIENCE

What is consciousness? Are we the products of our environment? Does consciousness come from us or does our environment influence it? Can we change our environment? Can we change our consciousness? Scientists and mystics are coming together to explore what is possible, what is probable. For example, since 1994 the University of Arizona has sponsored annual conferences on "The Science of Consciousness," which feature preeminent scientists and mathematicians as well as experts in spirituality and holistic/alternative health, such as Deepak Chopra, Stuart Hameroff, and Sir Roger Penrose.

In such gatherings we are finally seeing the merging of science and spirituality. Deepak Chopra, the late Wayne Dyer, Gregg Braden, Nassim Haramein, and others have shown the meaningful merits of integrating science and spirit. The mainstream and peer-reviewed materials all agree that consciousness is connected and that, therefore, human life is connected to all of life. The true meaning of consciousness is not totally understood or agreed upon. Yet many scientists and philosophers alike agree that it is an inner experience based on the individual's subjective experiences. Everyone has inner awareness; however, some inner awareness may be the same or similar and some may not be the same. Thus it is both personal and universal. Many who experience what I call universal consciousness are able to see and feel pure truth, pure thought as perhaps coming from universal awareness. It is universal when researchers ask the same questions of persons under the influence of hallucinogens or hypnotherapy and receive similar answers. It is subjective when we color it with our biases and experiences. In addition, I believe consciousness is the source of life as we know it, and that universal ideas exist for all to access.

Consciousness isn't everything, but it is so much of what we have ignored that it is now getting front seat. When I was younger, I knew many more truths that were coming directly from consciousness. As you wake up, you too will see and know without knowing "why." Challenge the information. Note it in your journals. Ask for confirmation or validation. It will come.

CREATING HEAVEN ON EARTH

You are the container, and consciousness bubbles up from within you. You can have a narrow pipe or a giant-sized one. It's up to you. You can open it with your will, your intention. You can also close it with your fear, judgment, rage, disappointment, and other negative emotions.

Early in my spiritual work, I was shown how to ask for "a day of Heaven on Earth." You can too. Start with that. Make every day a good one by using a simple prayer: *I'm asking for a day of Heaven on Earth for me and everyone I come in contact with.* When I began, I realized I was typically envisioning a challenging day; then I corrected myself, humorously offering the replacement phrase, *I'm having a day of Heaven on Earth.* The results were astounding! After the third time I made this "affirmation" I realized that I could ask for it every day—and so can you!

VIEWS FROM OTHER TEACHERS

December 21, 2012, marked the completion of the Great Mayan Cycle and the beginning of a New World Age. I was selected to join Hunbatz Men, who originally wrote about the end of the Mayan calendar on the solstice in December 2012 at Chichén Itzá, the Mayan temple in the Yucatan, as a group of spiritual teachers and seekers to birth the new age. Hunbatz Men said, "Now is the time for the woman to lead as a spiritual teacher." Women will not be silenced. YET, it is more than that. It is the time of the divine feminine within you! And it is time for the balanced divine feminine and the balanced divine masculine in both men and women. Chapter 8 goes into this deeply.

This book isn't about what other people are doing to hold you back, or hold you up, even though that energy is real. Instead, consider that this book contains the keys to claiming your birthright, understanding your reality, and learning how to co-create a new version of Heaven on Earth. Each of you is discovering that the door is wide open, waiting for you to decide what to do next! Mainstream knowledge wants to perpetuate the status quo. Nothing in the universe will support that. Choose to be part of the new now, choose to show up and do your part and wake up in fifth dimension!

1

The Wake-Up Call to Fifth Dimension

The fifth dimension is a vibrational frequency of unconditional love with the absence of fear, where compassion rules your emotions. As mentioned in the prologue, the fifth dimension is what traditional religions teach is heaven. It is the next place humanity is moving and expressing through. Actually, much of humanity is already expressing in the fifth dimension.

Although we usually think of ourselves as being three dimensional, we are actually in a place slightly above the third dimension. Most of humanity is in this place, slightly more than halfway between third and fourth (3⅝ to be exact). This number may seem odd, but think of it simply as a measure: an elevator may stop at the third floor, or it may stop at a higher place than the third that is not yet the fourth!

All the dimensions are nested like Russian dolls. The fourth is different from the third, but you can simultaneously experience both. The fifth dimension is remarkably similar to the third, and you might not notice the difference at first. The higher up the dimensional experience you go, the more you are able to discern higher frequencies with a peaceful, soothing feeling. From this new vantage point (fourth or fifth dimension), you can experience the lower dimensions with grace, compassion, and dispassionate interest.

 PLAY "WHAT IF?"

Awareness of something that appears to be illogical is a good indicator that you are actually plugged into your fifth-dimensional self.

1. When this happens and you notice this illogical data, take time to connect with Mother Earth (grounding). You can do this quickly by sending an energetic "taproot" from your pranic tube exiting at the tail bone deep into Mother Earth.* Many shamanic traditions label this process as grounding.
2. Then allow a "what if" scenario to play out in your mind. Claim it is real, demand access, release your thoughts—and wait.
3. You will be surprised how quickly this will result in crystal-clear understanding and information.

One of the outcomes of this exercise is the abrupt shift of viewpoint into timelessness. This too is a magical experience if you accept that it is possible. Timelessness is usually accompanied by a sense of deep peace and a quality of compassion that defies explanation. Allow yourself to experience it. Note it. Wait until you've come to terms with it yourself before you talk about it.

WAKING UP DIFFERENT

Waking up is the recognition that the eternal now is all you have. Waking up in fifth dimension is different from your current form of waking up. This should be obvious, but for the sake of discussion it is useful to say so. You will find that your rest will become deeper and deeper as you

---

*The pranic tube is the energy tube that sits in front of the spine, running from one hand length above your head to one hand length below your feet, extending five to seven inches in either direction. It enters the body in the location of the original soft spot or crown chakra and exits at the perineum in both men and women. Normally, it is filled with the living energy, called prana, or life force.

become more fifth-dimensional. You may realize that you have trouble "waking up" in the morning or awakening from naps. This is real. This is a new function of waking up in fifth dimension. This is because you are going deeper, connecting with other versions of you, and waking up your inner awareness of who you really are!

For many in the West, waking up consists of being awakened from sleep by some sort of external alarm. Various kinds of alarms are part of the technology the body has gotten used to—disturbing people from their rest. Even so, many of you are now using your own inner clock to awaken you from sleep. Some of you are noticing that even if you do set an external alarm, you wake up before it goes off. Or some of you may have gravitated to the slow, easy wakeup of the "Om clocks" or light clocks that use a gentle light that grows brighter over a thirty-minute time period.

Certain alignments take place in the dreamtime that are essential to our ever-present now. When you wake yourself abruptly, either by an outside sound or by your choice of alarm, you disturb the process of moving your consciousness from higher planes to lower material expressions. Help yourself by choosing to slow down the wake-up process: allow your body to drift slowly into awareness from the dreamtime in order to bring your most evolved essence back into your body. This is your opportunity to maximize higher dimensional energies.

Your physical rest is your time away from the body. You also may be bringing in a better version of the body you have. I recommend the Triple Mantra meditation* as one tool that will aid you in doing this. Modern technology exists whereby one can rejuvenate. For example, Secret Space Program insider Corey Goode has released information on the Gaia TV network show *Cosmic Disclosure* sharing the impressive array of technology, such as rejuvenating machines, withheld from humanity. As one military insider informed me, if you (Maureen) know about it, it means the military has had this tech-

---

*See Suggested Resources for more on this meditation.

nology for twenty-five to fifty years. This type of knowledge has been withheld from most humans, but it doesn't matter. You may go around this blockade and use your mind to tap into whatever "systems" might be appropriate for you. You don't even need to know they exist or how they exist. Advanced technology exists for healing, manufacturing, replication, and more. For our purposes this might include technology to heal the body. You can imagine that in your mind too. Imagine there is a machine that heals whatever ails you and one that can bring you to the futuristic location where this healing takes place, such as on a spaceship or healing center in a secret location in the dreamtime. You can access this technology from a higher dimension, imprint it into the energy body, and then let it produce physical outcomes. Keeping a journal of your circumstances and of the changes you observe will help you appreciate your progress. Do not be discouraged. You are all becoming masters at whatever you are passionate about. You are having fun—and if you aren't—you probably need to find out what's going on!

CHANGE YOUR PERCEPTION

This book is also a part of your fifth dimension wake-up call! We are being called to be aware of what is possible, what our true inheritance is, and how to claim it. This book will guide you through this process and help you understand and organize your efforts.

This book seeks to *change your perception of what is possible.* Over and over, throughout the book, I'll include this phrase to help point out where you may be tempted to stay in a belief system or behavior that is based on our historical experiences, and not what is possible. Notice that I didn't say old or outdated belief system. Once you are in fifth dimension, belief systems just are, because there is no polarity, no preference or derogation. Once you've changed your concept of what's possible, you've altered your course forever and the course of humanity right along with it.

WHAT CAN KEEP YOU OUT OF THE FIFTH DIMENSION?

All seekers require understanding about what keeps you out of fifth dimension.

One of the most important circumstances that keeps you out of fifth dimension is not getting enough sleep. In fact you may need much more sleep than you may think is necessary. Longer sleep times take you deeper and deeper into your fifth dimensional expression. This is because during these deeper rest periods you are able to recalibrate with your higher vibrational self which allows you to maintain your fifth dimensional self while waking.

Energetic Blocks and Disruptors

There are many outside disruptors that can impact your ability to stay in 5D. They include chemtrails, which are manufactured chemical releases from high-flying jets that have deleterious effects on life on this planet,* and both direct and indirect vibrational influences. Direct influences include cell phones, wireless Internet, and other electronic devices of all kinds. Indirect influences include programming being beamed from various locations, along with food modifications and so on. Once you have activated your Higher Self connection, you will notice these energies and frequencies, while simultaneously experiencing them, thus allowing you to practice your discernment.

I once felt the field of energy from our wireless router literally follow me into bed and then into my ear. It felt like a hot wire probe was being pushed into my ear canal! I immediately got up from bed and disconnected the wireless router in my home. I got a timer for the router after that! How does excess router energy feel? You may have put your cell phone up to your ear and it actually hurt on the inside of your

---

*Much has been written about chemtrails; for more information you can see the blog post: http://floweroflifeblog.com/2015/10/ascended-masters-through-maureen-st-germain.

ear canal. That's exactly the same energy. Why sleep with the wireless router on? You turn the lights off—turn the router off too.

Don't Look Back

You may find yourself thinking about a situation in the past and trying to identify whether it was a fifth dimensional experience or a third dimensional experience. Please know that your desire to know this is commendable, albeit counterproductive! Why? Because the need to know about your past in order to evaluate it actually keeps you locked in third dimension! Why?

Examine your purpose. Are you evaluating and judging yourself? Self-reflection is of course an important part of mastery. However, trying to decide whether a behavior was fifth dimensional or third dimensional is using your mind, not your heart. To establish anything strictly for the sake of evaluation is a third dimensional act, linked to ego. Do yourself a favor and pay attention to your now. When you do this, the fifth dimension will take care of itself.

Understand that your ego is your friend, does a good job, but isn't always right! Your ego is looking after you. Your ego wants you to be safe and happy. How does the ego do this? It uses the past to evaluate the possible choices in front of you! Spending your life sorting out good or bad may have been useful to you in the third-dimensional version of reality, since it was based on polarity. However, now that we are all moving into 5D pretty regularly, using the old system of categorizing experiences based on their historical impact on you prevents you from being in the present moment and locks you into 3D's polarity-based grip. Be in the present, and your 5D actions and energies will hold you in alignment there.

The Need to Replace Old Beliefs

If you don't take charge of your future, someone else will! Our future was hijacked once, by beings that thought they knew better as expressed in the many versions of Earth's prehistory being released for our edification. Two such versions can be found in *Entangled* by Graham Hancock and *Confessions of a Rebel Angel* by Timothy Wyllie. Each of these sources is other worldly. Both books have more than my comfort level of violence (I usually skip over these parts), yet they show us our prehistory from differing vantage points and invite us to consider our prehistory with a little more compassion.

That was a long time ago, and we've come a long way since that time. However, there are a few such beings lingering around, who are still attempting to control you through fear and manipulation. But you can stand firm against them if you decide now, once and for all, that you are a being of light and nothing will ever hold you back again.

It is high time for us to embrace our fullest potential; and in light of the past depicted in these types of books, we can begin to see that potential is really, really great! It's also about a certain level of discovery, the "waking up" into our full, fifth-dimensional expression. Gautama Buddha was asked by a visitor, "Are you a God?" "No, I'm just awake," was his loving reply. When you wake up in fifth dimension, are you God? Nope. You're just awake.

I mention these discoveries for a purpose, which is to help you own the fact that all you know is not enough; it is to help you expect new and different beliefs to replace those treasured belief systems you've held from the past. This cannot happen unless you recognize that your current beliefs are based on a third-dimensional reality, which has nearly no reference point from fifth-dimensional reality. In a small way, it is like learning a foreign language. First you learn a few words—and think you can talk—until you realize you must give up your way of constructing a sentence! Then you grow your vocabulary. Along the way you will enjoy similarities, but they may be few and far between. You will even find that some 5D ways will be simply inexplicable in third-dimensional thinking.

Everywhere around you, there are those who cannot or will not challenge the overlord system that has held humanity back. This system consists of secret governments with agendas that make people feel as though they have no other option but to follow along with the status quo in third-dimensional living. They are convinced they have no choice and sadly are simply ill-informed. By picking up this book and applying the knowledge within, you can change everything. People who consider the possibility that they can change reality become empowered, knighted if you will, by Source to make a difference. Consider that what is possible is still being discovered and uncovered.

HOW TO OPTIMIZE YOUR WAKE-UP

In fifth dimension you will learn to practice discernment, not judgment. No longer will you need to compartmentalize information into good or bad or create comparisons.

Seeing the Beauty in Everything

Looking for beauty everywhere is one of the first steps in becoming fifth dimensional. Start looking for it where you are. Look for it in nature; surprise yourself with this newfound joy of seeing beauty everywhere.

Gratitude and Presence

Being in a place of deep gratitude about everything will assist you in achieving a permanent 5D state. Allowing yourself to be fully in the present moment will also assist you in achieving high states. Yet there is something to be said about observing your happiness, observing your gratitude while staying in the now.

After I had conducted a particularly "high" class years ago, my host and I were discussing the wonderful experience while having breakfast on her front porch. We could hear the birds singing—sweetly and loudly. My host commented that she didn't ever remember so many birds singing so sweetly and loudly before. Then our thoughts turned to more mundane elements of the workshop that were less than perfect. Suddenly, it was as if someone flipped a switch, and once again we noticed the birds. This time, it was their silence. They had stopped singing! That's when we realized we were initially holding such a high vibration (5D) that they matched our energies; thus, their original chorus was so substantially joyful. When we lowered our thoughts to the "complaints" we had about the workshop and ourselves, their singing stopped. What a wake-up call!

DEVELOP YOUR CONNECTION WITH YOUR HIGHER SELF

If it feels like you are not in the fifth dimension, you can ask for help. Ask your Higher Self to bring you people/situations that will boost your frequency. The Higher Self Practice will help you to turn trust into knowing. Don't delude yourself into thinking you already have a healthy connection to your Higher Self. Instead, take the six-week challenge; only then can you check in everything you are learning with your own Higher Self. Please do this for yourself, for your own mastery. Take your Higher Self connection to the next level so that you can know what you need to know all the time. A succinct version is given here, and a full explanation can be found in my book, *Beyond the Flower of Life* (listed in Suggested Resources at the end of this book).

✳ HIGHER SELF PRACTICE

In this practice you will ask questions of your Higher Self while holding to the following seven agreements for a set period of time, which ideally is at least six weeks. Start with a heart centered meditation asking what symbols or signals from your Higher Self will indicate "yes," "no," and neutral."

1. Select a time frame. This is called your practice period. It should be no less than forty-five days. It could be longer. Decide what your practice

period future end date is. If today is June 1, then July 15 is the end of your practice period.

2. Ask only yes or no questions. No open-ended questions.

3. Ask unimportant, insignificant questions, ones that you do not care about the outcome of, such as "Should I take this route to get to work?" or "Should I wear the red shirt?" If you are asking about what to wear, for example, keep asking new questions until you get a "yes." Ask unimportant questions throughout the day as often as thirty to fifty times.

4. Always follow through with the answer you are given. No exceptions. This is to keep the practice period clear. After your practice period, if you decide not to follow your Higher Self, it is OK—but you will probably regret it.

5. Do not ask important questions. If you absolutely cannot defer asking a specific question until after your forty-five days, then make an exception. Make exceptions rare.

6. Do not ask predictive questions, such as, "Will the traffic light change before I get there?" or "Will the phone ring in the next few minutes?" These type of questions are inviting your ego to track your progress. If you are tracking your progress, then you still care about the outcome. (See agreement 3.)

7. Do not use any forms of divination during your practice period. Do not use kinesiology, muscle testing, finger testing, cards, or pendulums. Divination has its place and can be useful, but not during your practice period. If you are a therapist and use these methods with your patients, limit their use to that practice. As far as you are concerned, only ask your Higher Self during this practice period.

Many times people think they are receiving good Higher Self information, but they just don't trust it. Your first communication from the Higher Self might be in body confirmations. The traditional one that almost everyone gets is goose bumps or goose flesh. One of my students consistently has gotten a strong metallic taste on her tongue whenever her Higher Self is present. Others might get a salty taste. It's a way for your body to tell you that you are in resonance with the divine version of you, your Higher Self.

No request can go unfilled. If you persist in asking for your Higher Self to communicate with you and you are specific that you want only your Higher Self, then your Higher Self will answer this call sooner or later. Be patient. Sometimes your Higher Self's signal is very subtle. Sure, you'd like it louder. But you must crawl before you run! So be gentle with yourself if you feel like your Higher Self is too faint. It will grow stronger, as will your ability to "sense" it. You can also acknowledge the faint feeling while asking for it to be stronger.

Eventually your Higher Self will be able to communicate with you through all means, such as sound (for example, a voice speaking in your head); smell or touch (you may smell or feel subtle energies moving in your body); or feeling (you may have a mild sensation of nausea or dizziness).

After your six weeks of practice, your ego will want to be "best friends" with your Higher Self because it will know and understand that the Higher Self will keep you safe. Your Higher Self is not better than you. It simply is a tremendous resource for your best and highest choices. You do not need to always follow your Higher Self. Yet, once you have this connection, you'll always choose it. Why? Well, the first time you don't follow your Higher Self wisdom, you'll wish you had in hindsight. All it takes is one time. After that, it's all about ego. Your ego wants you to be safe and get what you want.

The result of learning the Higher Self connection is that when you ask your Higher Self a question, you don't have to trust your Higher Self's answer. You just know your Higher Self can only provide accurate information in the moment. I know of no other process that will give you 100 percent accuracy, which is needed so you can know, not trust, but know what you need to know. This is not a matter of faith, but connection.

ACTIVATE THE POWER OF
ASSERTION, PROTECTION, INTENTION

When you find yourself getting bumped from fifth dimension, remember that you belong in 5D! You can try these tools to claim your right to fifth dimension. Say, "You have no power over me." or "You don't scare me." You'll be amazed at how these simple statements—even while spoken in an empty room—when you are feeling overwhelmed or overpowered, will make a huge difference. A nice Epsom salts bath will also go a long way toward releasing unwanted vibrations! Another tool is the wonderful stone known as shungite. Put a chunk of this powerful stone into your bath water to release heavy or dark energies.

You can also set up an energetic "Faraday cage" around your bed. A Faraday cage is an enclosure used to block electric fields, usually formed by conductive material or by a mesh of such materials. In this exercise, you set up an energetic protection for yourself so you can sleep peacefully at night and truly recharge with the energy of your Higher Self.

 ### SETTING UP A FARADAY CAGE

1. Put your hands on your heart. Move them away from your body—like you are pulling a thread (or channel) from your heart.
2. Now let your hands become completely open and outstretched, as you imagine that you are creating a "Faraday cage" around your bed. Intend that it remain in place until you awaken in the morning.
3. Be sure to do this every night. At some point it will become permanent.

You may also find your way by monitoring your awareness and setting your intention. Make a clear intention as you drift off to sleep, such as this:

Dear God, Angels, and Guides, I request to attend the most evolved place I may move to with my consciousness, for the purpose of clarity about my mission, my purpose, and service. Let me learn and understand better what I need (to know, learn, and be) to achieve my fullest potential. Assist me in any upgrades that may be possible. Thank you, Amen.

HELPING WITH JOY, PATIENCE, AND HONESTY

Choose to be helpful and joyful. Make it your purpose to follow through on anything that you are attracted to. Remember your musings, visions, and dreams, and write them down. Ask for guidance on what they might mean.

••

MAKE IT YOUR PURPOSE TO FOLLOW THROUGH ON IDEAS, ACTIONS, AND THOUGHTS TO WHICH YOU ARE ATTRACTED.

••

Do your best to be honest with yourself right away. Make a commitment to always tell the truth, and then ask your angels and guides* to help you notice when you are not honest with yourself! You'll find yourself laughing to yourself when you (or your angels) "catch" you. You can get used to living the truth of what you are, imperfections and all. In the world of the twelve-step recovery program, honesty is the key to self-mastery. These groups of recovering individuals are the "leaders of the pack" for this honesty. This openness needs to be practiced with your close friends and family.

Indeed, secretiveness or any other form of withholding will fall away in fifth dimension. But it is important to be gentle with others. When asked a question, be sure to be truthful, yet simple. You can only change

---

*Your angels are beings from the angelic creation, not Earth, that were created to bring God's love to humanity and produce miracles to make it possible to feel the love of God. Your guides are unseen helpers who have a specific connection to the Earth, often due to their having lived on the Earth and achieving a specific mastery. They come to help you with your progress by instructing you in your meditations and dreamtimes and support you as you seek wisdom, balancing, and heart opening.

yourself. When you encounter someone who is interested in your new and different experiences, share what works for you only when asked a second time—not on the first request, but the second. The first request for information or understanding is where the other person's mind is open. They are noticing you are different and may be curious. Don't ruin the opportunity by being too quick to share your new experiences and scaring them away when only their mind is open. The time will come when you will be able to let your true self be known. In this way you remove the façade gently.

The second time people ask is when their hearts have opened. This is when they are ready to react to your information and truly take it in and discover its value. Remember to give them a simple, nonthreatening answer the first time, like, "Well, I had a great weekend attending a seminar on personal growth. Let's go ahead and order lunch." After your simple, nondisclosure answer, change the subject. This may seem contradictory, but preaching is never needed in fifth dimension. When they come back to you for advice or information, then and only then is it appropriate to sincerely express your new wisdom and express who you are instead of hiding it.

You will be shown ways to change your thinking, behavior, and communication by selectively adding to your vocabulary and consciously eliminating words that divide, while adding words that are descriptive yet nonpolarized.

Next, offer some of your kindness and compassion to the competitor who may be your collaborator tomorrow. Do not insist that your way is the right way or yours is the only way, because of course it is not. There is no right way. In fifth dimension there is no right or wrong! There is only that which pleases you now.

As you begin to own the statement—that your way is one possibility of many—you will then be able to feel it internally as well as speaking it yourself with great grace and ease. And you can add this to your communications by responding to any new idea with the opening remark, "Consider the possibility . . ." This is your new now.

• •

INSTEAD OF A COMPETITION, THE NEW GAME IS A DANCE!
YOU CAN DANCE ALONE, BUT IT'S MORE FUN (AND MORE
APPROPRIATE) WITH A PARTNER OR TWO!

• •

CAN ANYONE DO THIS?

Think about how you spend your nonrecreational time, how you spend your work or efforts—whether paid or not—and decide from this point forward to always do more than what is expected. Your rewards will follow. This is how you make an investment in your future. When you exercise your willpower and determination, you begin to change your direction. The universe will support this.

Decide to change your perception of what is possible. Learn to think in a different way. How do you do that? Imagine that when you go to work, you put on a "work hat." Maybe you come home to a partner or children; that's your "Mom or partner hat." Initially, you are giving yourself permission to think differently in various situations. This will eventually lead to "allowing" new ways of thinking to emerge, because you are not stuck on "the way you always do things." Learn to admit your mistakes to yourself and others. As hard as it may seem, it's better to train yourself and your friends to get used to speaking the truth when you discover your mistakes—when you discover that you would do it differently next time.

Learn to refine your goals. Just when you think you are doing okay is about the time you can improve. This is not the same as second-guessing and holding yourself up to some unnamed standard all the time.

Pray for Your Neighbor

Many authors, including me, have written about believing in yourself. Now it's time to believe in both you and your neighbor. Create an air of optimism. Create an air of joyful allowing. Remember to pray both for yourself and your competition. Better that you both get wisdom.

Wisdom creates solutions and smoothness. *Fun* and *flexibility* are the new "f-words" of fifth dimension. Decide your competition is your ally; you just haven't figured out how yet.

Don't wish things were easier. Instead, ask that things get better for everyone. Not only do dancers rely on each other, they rely on mutual support to achieve something greater than themselves. Treat partners as if they were your dance partners—knowing that whatever befalls them impacts you as well—and in this way, you benefit from your partner's good fortune! Think of how wonderful our world would be when everyone is praying for everyone else as well as himself or herself!

If your partner, relative, friend, or coworker is mean or inconsiderate, respond as if he or she were your favorite person! Can you imagine if your dear friend wrote a "must be nice . . ." text as a vote of approval and loving teasing? Within minutes you receive a similar remark from a stranger that could be misperceived as a jealous comment or insult. Why not treat both remarks the same, with laughter and joy? You get to choose how you receive any message. We were put here to exercise our abilities as co-creators. Now is the time to make magic.

A coworker shared with me how he had sold his very high-end sports car to his son at a considerable discount from what he was expecting to get from the sale of this car. He explained ruefully that his son had talked him into letting it go for about half of what the co-worker hoped to get in the marketplace. I smiled and looked at him, my eyes shining, and said, "Just think about how proud you would be of your son if he had gotten that same deal from a stranger!" He looked confused, then shocked for a moment before he burst out laughing! Yes, that applies to all of us.

There is one exception. It is when someone has broken his or her agreement with you. When someone fails to do his or her part, you are not obligated to fulfill your side. During the "old days" in the legal arena, breach of contract voided the contract. Today, however, many contemporary agreements include a clause that actually says, "Failure of one part of this contract does not void any other part of the contract."

This clause is included to protect the party who is providing the service and limits liability. While I'm not suggesting you break a legally signed contract, there are many examples where an "implied" contract is not fulfilled and you most certainly can and should exercise your right to decline to do your part as well. Or at the very minimum, you should examine how you feel about it and choose to honor it—not because you want to look like a good guy (ego based), but because it pleases you in the moment.

In this true story, a little old lady from Boston kept asking her taxi driver to go slower, as he was driving too fast through heavy traffic to the airport. They finally arrived. Worse for the wear and tear of the crazy ride, she paid and walked away. He called after her, "Hey, lady, where's my tip?" She marched back toward him, got close, and punched him in the nose. "That's your tip!" she announced angrily. Hearing this story from my friend about her seventy-nine-year-old mother right after I had relayed a similar story about a taxi driver, who had overcharged me, intrigued me. I asked in meditation why these two stories had come together in this moment, and I was shown that I also shouldn't have given a tip—that my tipping was tied to my ego around being a good person. You need to understand and respect yourself enough to do what's appropriate in the moment and not let your ego drive your actions!

The Brakes Have Come Off

Notice how birds land on a branch—with absolute trust. They trust that the branch will move with them as they land and then stabilize. You can do the same. What if your "landing" isn't what you expected and you wobble? Does that mean you will fall? Hardly! Even gymnasts land in a way that forces them to deal with their weight and forward movement. You are strong and can do the same. Recognizing that movement when you land is normal is a helpful ability. Change is your new now, and you are adding your experiences and understanding of human nature to your circumstances. Everything is in flux. The brakes have come off, but that doesn't mean you'll do it all at once. You will learn, practice, push limits, and keep going farther, faster. The time is now for expansion of a vastness that is greater than you have ever imagined.

WAVES OF LOVE

Humanity is being bombarded with tremendous support to change. It's an odd thing that this energy gently affects you, yet could affect you greatly if you invite it to do so. You are part of the system of third dimension that is changing. You are either ahead of the curve, in the middle, or behind it. It's more fun to be at the front of the wave, as there is an easy push, especially when you know it's coming. Have you ever stood at the seashore without looking and with your back to the waves? Probably only once! It's not fun getting knocked down by a wave that you didn't see coming. Yet you could choose to let the wave push you to shore, just as a surfer rides the wave. There are many new tools coming your way. The new 5D MerKaBa featured in a later chapter is one of the tools.

This energy is being broadcast all around you. It has come in to assist you, to anchor the higher vibrations into your body with grace and ease. Ask to easily receive and integrate the most evolved vibration possible for you this day. Do it daily. Do it like this:

Dear God, May I gently and gracefully shift and change with the energies made available for me this day.

2
How We
Process Information

Here is where you begin to change your perception of what is possible!

In Jonah Lehrer's best seller, *How We Decide,* he tells us that ever since the times of the ancient Greeks, the single theme about how we think and decide is based on the idea that humans are rational. He then explains that's not how the brain works and further discloses that humans were not meant to be only rational creatures. He asserts that our emotions play an important part of the process. His concern is that, "Despite the claims of many self-help books, intuition isn't a miraculous cure all. . . . The simple truth of the matter is that making good decisions requires us to use both sides of the mind."[1]

That is to say, we need to find the balanced and ideal use of emotions and logic. Science and the new spirituality share this important theme. Moving into 5D is actually the merging of both mental and emotional processing of information. It is the merging of logical, linear thinking with an emotional response to the environment. You need to learn how to use both your emotions and your mind to help you evolve as a human being and become fifth-dimensional.

DIFFERENT WAYS OF THINKING

The difference between the third dimension and fifth dimension is the way that they work. Awareness of the distinction between linear

26

thinking, multilinear thinking, and dynamic thinking leads you down the path of self-awareness that will take you to a perceptible shift in consciousness. I'll start with the differences between linear and non-linear, and then we can explore multiple linear and dynamic thinking to help you begin developing an understanding of what to expect in 5D.

Linear thinking may be distilled to cause and effect. Many people are still taught that everything is based on cause and effect, and that rational thinking based on logic is the only valid expression of enlightened thought. This belief exists in spite of the radical awareness of quantum physics that began in the early 1900s with the work of Max Planck. Remember that special phrase I promised to include at pivotal moments? Here it is again: It's time to change your perception of what is possible.

Linear thinking tends to be very polarized although not always. Compartmentalizing situations, people, or experiences is linear. Linear thinking can be explained by the relationship that distance equals velocity times time. We use this equation without noticing when we drive on the freeway and want to figure out how long it will take to get from one location to another. There is a direct proportional relationship between one side of the equation and the other. If you double the speed, you halve the time it takes to reach your destination. Linear thinking always creates a straight line when plotted on a graph. Logic is built from linear thinking.

Another way to look at linear systems is to examine time. Scientists and mystics alike agree that time cannot be measured. The only element of time that really exists is the present moment. This is the ever present now. We pretend that the past exists because we have memory, because we have books, because we have writing, and so on, but in truth the past does not exist until we reexperience it. It is simply a memory. Sometimes we have a record of it, as in an audio or video recording, diaries or journals, and history books. The past, along with potential futures, is recorded in the Akashic Records (see the boxed explanation on page 28). This is why you can change the past as well as the future.

What Are the Akashic Records?

This is the energy field of all that is. It was created after creation, when it was felt that a record of the activity in consciousness might be of interest. This is an energy field that exists in the eleventh dimension, unaffected by human interaction, although it records human interaction. It is vibrationally dissimilar to the third, fourth, fifth dimensions, and so on. Tuning to the records or readings is a vibrational shift, so that the vibration of your seeking wisdom matches the vibration of the records. There is a very specific spiritual dispensation that allows one to do this, much like a tunnel under a body of water lets you cross the expanse without actually entering any of the area surrounding it. When one "reads" the records, they are generally not actually going into the energetic field; rather they are communing with guides who are actively assigned to the region of the records being explored. This is done through the vibrational match that occurs. Some of the Akashic Records guides rotate in service, and others are permanent members of the Akasha. The guides may be likened to large genderless energy beings that actually hold information in their consciousness. The closest description that can be given is that they resemble the travelers, the special beings who transported people through space portals, in the movie and book, *Dune*.

Many believe that time is the fourth dimension. Although that may be one possibility, it is not the one I know. Time is so misunderstood that I've developed an entire chapter on this information (see chapter 7).

Comparing Linear Time with a Multiple-Linear Timeline

Until now, we have been "programmed" to see only one version of reality. Modern physics teaches multiple versions of reality. Multiple possibilities exist with each decision we make, but because the brain has been locked into the pattern of registering only one version of an experience (even if one sees more than one), it tends to dismiss this possibility. You are already choosing multiple paths but do not notice. Many physicists have postulated on the multiple versions of reality and believe this explains quantum mechanics. Some physicists go so far as to say that more than one reality actually exists, like branches on a tree, never intersecting.* My guides tell me that each reality worthy of your experience is played out. Now you can notice and observe without judgment. This is a big game changer.

Looking linearly, you can look backward in time and trace a straight line from your now to a past moment. For example, let us say that you graduated from a specific nursing school. Before that, you may have graduated from college. Before that, you graduated from high school, and before that you graduated from eighth grade, and so on. This is a linear process because you're following a straight line in a sequence of events, albeit backward in time. You are using linear thinking to look backward in time at your history of individual choices.

By reversing this view and examining time from the vantage point of the past, you can begin to comprehend a multiple-linear view. When you were in eighth grade looking to the future, you may have considered attending more than one high school. After high school you may have applied to more than one college (or advanced training). Finally, after college you may have considered multiple graduate schools. As you look at all of these choices, at every juncture you can conclude that multiple choices existed. Although not limitless, they gave a variety of options to consider.

The future doesn't exist from the vantage point of "now" but can be considered as one of multiple possibilities that we may experience or are likely to experience. This process of looking forward into the multiple possibilities in the time-space continuum is a multiple-linear vantage point. Each possibility is experienced by the value or weight you put on it. This is explained further in chapter 7.

---

*This is represented by the quantum-mechanical "Schrödinger's cat" theorem, according to the many-worlds interpretation. In this interpretation, every event is a branch point; the cat is both alive and dead, but the "alive" and "dead" cats are in different branches of the universe, both of which are equally real, but which do not interact with each other.

Dynamic Systems

Dynamic systems appear to be linear, yet randomly jump out of their predictability. A small snowball rolling downhill at some point will collect enough snow to cause an avalanche. The avalanche occurs when critical mass is achieved and a large enough ball of snow brings the mountain of snow down. Differences may show up unexpectedly and randomly. Science has labeled this "chaos."

Perhaps you remember the child's game "pick up sticks," where a bunch of slender sticks of the same size are released upright on a table like a bunch of sharpened pencils. They are allowed to fall into a pile onto the table, and the children take turns picking them up. The game begins when the first child picks up a stick without disturbing the pile. Each child takes a turn picking up a stick without disturbing the pile. This continues until one unlucky child picks up a stick that causes the pile of sticks to shift, and she is cast out of the game. This game exhibits the apparent order plus randomness that describes what we call non-linear or dynamic systems.

USING THE DYNAMIC VIEW

You may access any timeline—both past and future—any time you want using specialized tools such as guided meditations, shamanic work, past or future regressions, and Akashic Records work. There are many ways to access the Akashic Records field. I teach a specific method for this inner work (for oneself) or service work (opening another person's records), which is available to anyone who wishes to learn. This ability to look at an event from multiple possibilities releases you from 3D. For example, certain phrases lock you into 3D: "My keys are missing. Someone stole them." Or: "I must have misplaced them." However, another way of looking at the same occurrence opens you up to 5D: "My keys are missing—I wonder what's going on?" The last example allows for all possible choices to be known. This may include multiple versions of the expressions, opening up incredible insight into the nature of reality and the nature of choice.

For example, maybe you chose to divorce, but had regret about all you might be missing, so you put a certain percentage of your energy in the choice not taken. What if you did choose both choices? Quantum physicists are currently grappling with this concept and named it "the collapse model, because they assume the moment you "choose" (to observe yourself) in a selection," all other possibilities collapse into the observed one. However, it is very likely that other versions of yourself are experiencing the other choice in an alternate reality! I have personally experienced more than one version of the reality simultaneously, expressing opposing choices. You can too.

Consider the possibility that every choice is actually a "road taken." What if you are already choosing both sides of a fork in the road? Perhaps wisdom can be found by realizing the one you choose to experience is your now. The other "choice" becomes another version of reality!

Escape from Repeated Patterns

Understanding the dynamic view means that when repeated patterns surface, you can choose to do something different. If you always react the same way to a situation, you are locked into 3D. Train yourself to notice when you are making comparisons and then decide to ask the question, "What's going on?" For most seekers, your desire to understand is limited by your mind's desire to compartmentalize information into a linear way of thinking. Once you realize this, you can decide to do something different. Compartmentalizing is one way to stay in 3D. Being open to possibilities is a way to be 5D. Noticing is the key to unlocking 5D.

Changing the Future with Surprising Insights

Several years ago, my husband, a physicist and fire science investigator, was involved in a fire case that happened aboard a freighter on the Atlantic Ocean. He traveled overseas several times to where the ship was docked. His job was to determine the cause of the fire. A month or so into this project, I started having visions of him being hit from behind by a steel beam. It felt deliberate and fatal. I was able to determine the location. It was definitely happening overseas. I was even able to pinpoint the timeline—some four months in the future. I was unsure of what to do with this information. I usually check in with my Higher Self on whether to even work with this type of insight. I check in to be certain that alerting someone to this sort of thing is appropriate. What were the implications?

Finally I confided in a staff member who often received "advance warnings" on my behalf. We were both stunned to discover that she was getting similar information. I had been ready to approach my husband for a while, but this added some urgency! I asked him if he had "checked in with his Higher Self" about returning to the ship. He caught me completely by surprise with his answer and said, "If you tell me there is some reason to not go back, like I would be in jeopardy, then I would not return." I told him of my visions. He asked me to open the Akashic Records for him. I was willing to do this. What happened next surprised both of us.

I was expecting him to raise questions like, "Is this real? Is my life in jeopardy? Is this future changeable?" Once in the Akashic Records, his first question was, "What caused the fire?" Until now, he had not talked about his investigation, and I really knew nothing about the fire. I thought he would be seeking personal information about himself and his life, so I didn't anticipate the question. Through me, the record keepers responded clearly and quickly, "There were two fires set to cover up a couple of murders." Not expecting that, I stopped, pulled back from the energy of the Akashic Records, and said to my husband, "That's very odd, since no one died in this fire!" My husband grimly looked at me and said, "Actually three people died in the fire." The record keepers continued with the explanation—that one fire was a "smoke screen" set to cause a lot of smoke and confusion while the other one was set to cause damage and eject one of the bodies. There was more to the gruesome story, as it related to a mob-type incident and cover-up.

We were in the Akashic Records several weeks later asking for more information on this subject and were told we could clear the assassin (of a dark discarnate entity that made him so skillful), and this action would dramatically change the reality, because this entity provided the assassin's accuracy. We did our part to clear the unknown individual. We were told later (through our clearing team*) that it had a ripple effect, which nullified his ability to do any "job" that involved a target.

I checked in (with my Higher Self) and learned it was okay for my husband to return a few more times to the ship. One month before the critical time, my husband, still with no scientific evidence for the cause of the fire, reported to the attorney in charge of the investigation that his wife, a psychic, had reported the above story to him! I do not consider Akashic Records work psychic and object to this terminology; however, it is commonly understood language that provides a way to explain an "other-worldly" source. Originally, the company, whose attorneys had hired him, had been accused of a faulty chemical container and was seeking scientific proof as to whether their container had caused the fire.

I questioned my husband about submitting that information. For years, my first husband had labeled me a flake, and I was amazed that my current physicist and expert witness husband was quoting our Akashic Records session to the lawyers that had hired him! He reminded me that in the world of investigation, especially when natural causes are missing, a psychic's information might be used to help clear up a case.

Shortly thereafter he was released from the case. The work was almost done, and the other fire investigators completed the final report. We don't know if the accused firm was given a message to "just settle and don't investigate further" or not, but I have a feeling the Akashic Records information was not the only source to imply foul play.

---

*Our clearing team can be found at www.ClearingEnergy.org. In my book *Reweaving the Fabric of Your Reality,* you will find the types of energies and entities a person can clear and ways to clear yourself, as well as how and why to hire an outside person or team of persons to do clearing for you. Additionally, the website listed above explains this in detail.

Changing the Past

In past-life work, it is possible to change a past decision that has plagued you in this lifetime. As we are winding up this cycle of 3D experiences, multiple timelines are being merged as we become fifth dimensional. There are multiple groups of timelines, all based on their relationship to one another. All of this is occurring in the background. There are personal and collective timelines. They might include your soul family timeline and groups you belong to including the collective humanity timeline. All changes you make affect everyone in that group. In addition, you can affect the future as you shift and change by understanding and utilizing this book.

When you become multidimensional, you may have inklings of this. You may be aware of it in the dreamtime or meditations. You might be able to do this work on your own; however, ideally you will have an expert in past-life regression who understands this principle of transforming the past to produce remarkable changes in this life. After a session (to transform a past life, for example), you literally have the ability to move into new unexpressed directions because some poor choice of the past has been mitigated. In this type of session work, you can be regressed back to the pivotal point of a choice and make a different choice. For example, a man who became a gunslinger and died in a gun-fight in a past life always picks a fight with people in this life for no apparent reason. In his session, he might decide to go live with his aunt after his mother dies, instead of hanging out at saloons with his father, becoming a gunslinger and losing to a much better opponent at the very young age of sixteen. After this work, he wouldn't have this same strong urge to be adversarial in his interactions with people. This form of past-life regression can allow you to change your past while under hypnosis. All of humanity is merging and compressing timelines as we move through this cycle toward becoming 5D. It is important to know and come to terms with the fact that multiple expressions of you can move about in multiple parallel timelines, heal the past, and thereby change your present and future! The timelines are collapsing as we move into fifth dimension and fewer versions of the experiences and timelines are needed. Thus the motivation exists to heal and transform the more painful versions of experience. There are specialists in this area of healing. They can help you if you are plagued by a past-life event that seems to be adversely influencing your current one, even if you do not know what it is.

In a simpler version of this type of experience you might be telling a story about something difficult that happened to you in the past that you haven't shared in a while. You might not notice a change while you are in the act of telling about this experience, but then, when you are lying in bed that night, reflecting on your day, you might realize the version you told your new friend was softer, kinder, and more loving than you remember experiencing it. This is how you merge timelines by yourself. You have retold an experience, where the difficulty has been transformed and carries far less emotional pain and baggage.

MOVING BEYOND POLARITY

The most important thing to understand is that humanity as a whole is moving from a reality that includes polarity, or good versus evil, to a reality that is devoid of polarity. What does that mean? Why would we do that? Let's look at some practical reasons first; then we'll look at logistics.

The original purpose of third dimension was to explore the vast variety that polarity can provide. Just imagine the amazing variety we have explored around the extremes of polarity. This cycle has ended, and we are winding up the way we did things in third dimension. Things have changed, the rules have changed, and it's not the same game we've been playing for eons. This means that our way of thinking (good versus evil), our way of doing (one person above another), and our way of being (everyone for him- or herself) are changing.

Third dimension is still a "free will" zone. You still have the freedom to choose a God-centered choice, or a not-God-centered choice.

In third dimension you might label them good and bad. Why would I use these strange words? It is because from the fifth dimension there is no polarity, only love, which translates to a God choice. The absence of love is the not-God choice. In later chapters we will discuss the other dimensions, those that still have polarity and those that do not. This means that as you become more fifth dimensional it will be very clear the polarity game is over. In fifth dimension you will still have choice; only the not-God choice is no longer attractive or ultimately even available to you. This can be further explained by an example where given the chance to host someone you admire, of course you would say yes! The possibility of not accepting that opportunity does not occur to you. This is the equivalent of the God choice. How you host, what you will serve, and other decisions will still give you the ability to choose, to experience variety, but you will not choose to decline hosting your well-respected guest. There are many choices you can make that reflect the new *love only* energy that no longer requires the existence of karma.

This idea of no more karma is challenging for many. The absence of karma is a concept first delivered to me in 1995. At the time even I was astonished at the possibility. I had no idea what this meant or how it could even be. The first persons that I shared this important information with were trusted spiritual students and friends, and even they did not receive this news very well. As more and more students have been educated on how to open to the Akashic Records, they too have received the same message, "No more karma." It means that humanity is no longer bound by the rules of returning to life to experience the pain you may have inflicted or received. Even if you are willing to turn the other cheek, as Jesus was quoted as saying, what about all the other people? The guidance has been very clear, as in this recent message from the Akashic Records, *All of you, all of humanity is love, you are loved and you are lovable. People may judge one another, but that is not our way. We ask you to continue to keep your heart open and let others step into their place of joy and peace. They may need more time to understand it all; they will get it. Love you. When you take up too much polarity, you keep the polar-*

ity game engaged. Seek not to understand but to console. The way the game ends is when there are no more players. Then there is only love.

This book was written so you could step into your fifth dimensional expression purposefully. When you choose not to keep track of others and let go of the need for karma, you have become part of the solution. *No more karma* is one of the most significant shifts humanity is undergoing. This means reincarnation *with karma* is not occurring any more. This is the end of a cycle, the end of an age; no one is bound by the lesser patterns of the past, especially the sins of a past life.

Preference for God action or God choice will prevail. Free will won't need to continue in the same way it has by exploring the deepest, darkest shadow, as was possible in the polarity expression of third dimension. Those who do not want to give up the game (of polarity) certainly may stay behind. The new Earth is already moving into fifth dimension. She (Mother Earth) is waiting on humanity to be a vibrational match to the newer higher vibrational frequencies that are already available to those who choose this.

••

THE MOST IMPORTANT THING TO UNDERSTAND IS THAT
HUMANITY AS A WHOLE IS MOVING FROM A REALITY THAT
INCLUDES POLARITY, OR GOOD VERSUS EVIL, TO A REALITY
THAT IS DEVOID OF POLARITY.

••

Why Did We Choose to Be in a Polarity Reality in the First Place?

This question is not easily answered—yet there are answers. Humans are the only beings that have the capacity to hold both the light and the dark simultaneously. This unifying of polar energies into one being was so that Source could better understand the nature of the unfolding of creation. The goal was that the human would ultimately be able to choose the light, and merge the dark into the light.

Initially, advancing into a 5D perspective allows us to greatly expand all possible experiences. It allows us to have awareness of emotions and expands the experience of choice. You can begin to observe yourself in a neutral way and permit yourself to express from both sides of the equation, both the good guy and the bad guy (very likely being both), in order to expand your experiences. What if you were both the perpetrator and the victim in a war?

For example, in a meditation—a fifth-dimensional moment—I discovered that the man who had stolen $5,000 from me was another version of me! Whoa! So did he (that other version of me) make karma with me by stealing from me? I don't think so! This interaction was stressful and challenging. My guidance was to send him a letter and then to accept what he offered me. At the time, I was simply following guidance, without any idea where it would lead. His response was a check for a few hundred dollars.

Each step of the way, I discovered another piece of information, like a puzzle coming together. Ultimately what I learned in this case was that my connection with him had a purpose. We each had swung to an extreme around integrity, me being super rigid about keeping agreements, he being very loose about adjusting agreements without mutual consent! Our final interaction was one of great compassion, because I was guided to connect with him despite seeing no real purpose to it. It was most challenging for me to even consider reconnecting when I received yet another instruction from my guides. Nonetheless, by following guidance, he and I reconnected, and we inspired each other to move more toward the middle, he with more integrity, me with less rigidity in our beliefs and behaviors. We accomplished that.

Yes, but Look at All the Pain and Suffering on Earth!

In a free will zone we have permission and possibilities to make mistakes. We have the freedom to make a "God choice" or a "not-God choice." It's up to us. Creation wants to expand the possibilities of experiences. In spite of this, man's inhumanity to man was never anticipated. Consider contemplating this without judgment! There are many factors related to this that are the subject of numerous books. This book's focus does not explore the greater reasons of why we devolved to the place we have been. Yet it is important to understand that it certainly wasn't part of a divine plan! Accepting this as a real possibility helps you begin to see things that you couldn't (or wouldn't) see before.

When you accept there could be situations and circumstances that were set in motion by forces that were outside the basic operational rules, you can begin to use your mind and heart to move into compassion, and into the fifth dimension.*

THOSE WHO WOULD HOLD YOU BACK

For almost twenty years, while traveling and teaching I used the term "those who would have you fail" to describe the beings whose agendas were contrary to waking up in the fifth dimension, which is also known as the Ascension, or the expression of divine qualities, while still being in a physical body. I was guided to choose use of a phrase that does not name those who would have us fail. Names, even ones that were well known, would empower them. Remember this when you are tempted to name-call anyone! Resisting them versus avoiding them is a polarity expression of emotion that would "feed alligators," as some might say.

More recently, I've been given the term, "those who would hold you back." I wondered why. When I meditated on the change of terms, and what was behind it, I learned that it's not possible for anyone to fail

---

*I mentioned Wyllie's book, *Confessions of a Rebel Angel*, on page 14 in an earlier discussion of this type of information on the outside forces causing man's inhumanity to man. That is not the subject of our discourse here. I'm simply giving you a resource to learn more if this is of interest to you. Long before I ever discovered Wyllie's book, in a most profound meditation, it was made clear to me that no one—not even the Creator—was prepared for man's inhumanity to his fellow man. This was *not* part of any plan.

anymore! So much energy from the ascended hosts* and other nonphysical beings is here to support our transformation into fifth-dimensional beings that the phrase has morphed to "hold back" instead of "fail."

To grapple with this, imagine setting up a college trust fund for a child. The grandparents and relatives all contribute to it. They all remind her while she's growing up, "That money is yours at age forty unless you use it to go to college. Any money left over, you'll get when you graduate." What's the likelihood that young woman will finish college? Even with free will, the likelihood that she will attend and graduate is very high!

As you contemplate this, you can begin to see how reality has changed right in front of you. Again, let me remind you: change your perception of what is possible. Because the way things are is unlike anything before! You now have the full benefit of the Ascension upon you.

In a recent channeling from the Great Divine Director, an Ascended Master who holds the divine blueprint for humanity, through me, he states, "It is not possible to fail. Anyone who wishes to achieve mastery will succeed, regardless if they use tools and invoke help. Like a child learns to walk, they might use a chair to help themselves walk sooner, but they will learn to walk whether learned slowly or quickly."

YOUR NEW NOW

Fifth dimension is our next vibrational destination and where we are headed now. In fact, you've probably been pulsating back and forth between third and fifth already. This may be surprising to you. Fifth dimension is the platform of joy and bliss, the perfected human state,

---

*Ascended hosts include Ascended Masters and other cosmic beings in service to humanity. In Theosophy, Ascended Masters are believed to be spiritually enlightened beings who in past incarnations were ordinary humans but who have undergone a series of spiritual transformations originally called initiations. In some cases an Ascended Master has achieved perfection as a human being and life experiences have served as the initiations, allowing him or her to operate as a being who is benevolent to all of life. This is the Ascension into fifth dimension.

and much more. It is not the end of the line, as traditional religions describe heaven. It is, however, the end of the line in terms of separateness. From this point forward, we actually care about our fellow human beings as much as we care about ourselves. We care about our beloved Earth as much as we care about ourselves.

From fifth dimension expressions onward, we move more and more into *group consciousness or awareness* as it is often referred to. Another name for this experience is *oneness*, which implies we are all one. You may have had an experience of this already, as many have experienced oneness in their meditations. Yet there are greater and greater states of perception of this oneness; those perceptions shift and change as we evolve into higher and higher states of consciousness.

Abandon the Need to Know How or Why

When you examine a Queen Anne's lace flower* from a distance, it's just one flower in a field of many. As you close in on it and examine the stem, you can see how it branches out into fifty or more little stems, each of which has ten or more flowers. You begin to see that the Queen Anne's lace flower is more like a dynamic or fractal-like ever-expanding system. This is where you are. You are at the place in history where you can begin to understand that your abilities to imagine new and unthought-of outcomes are real and possible.

You have the ability to produce real and tangible different outcomes, even though you may not know how to use it yet. It is where you are going. Abandoning the need to know frees you from the linear process and allows you to "accept" information in a new way.

Abandoning the "how or why" is not the only way but is an important conscious tool to greatly expand your ability to achieve and become 5D. How do you do this? Notice when you are asking, "Why did X happen?" Notice your thought and decide to move into wonder. Do this by asking the question, "I wonder what's going on. . . ." *Wonder* is the

---

*Also known as wild carrot, sometimes confused with Bishop's flower.

replacement word for *why*. It will allow you to receive information that does not necessarily fit into your current 3D paradigm. That is one way you may expand into 5D thinking. The information, solution, or awareness will float easily to you, whether in the moment you ask the question, later in meditation, or in the dreamtime! Be prepared for surprises. Allow the unexplainable to be possible. Remember the phrase, It's time to change the perception of what is possible.

• •
FROM THIS VANTAGE POINT (THIRD DIMENSION),
THE MOMENT YOU EXPERIENCE YOUR TRUE IDENTITY, AS ONE
AND THE SAME AS ALL OF LIFE, IT MAY SEEM AS IF THAT'S ALL
THERE IS AND ALL THERE COULD BE. PAY ATTENTION TO THIS
PERSPECTIVE, AND IT WILL ALLOW YOU TO MOVE INTO GREATER
AND GREATER LEVELS OF MASTERY, BRINGING YOU INTO
YOUR PERMANENT STATE OF FIFTH DIMENSION.
• •

It's a Dance and the Heart Leads

It is important to note that you cannot be fifth dimensional without engaging your heart. There are some humans that were so wounded, at such an early age, that they developed the ability to activate their chakras above the heart while bypassing the heart chakra. They activated this ability as a matter of survival. I call them survival psychics.*

Survival psychics use their higher chakra gifts to get information and control their environment; they use this information with their minds. For them, it's about maintaining control. For them, it truly is a matter of life and death because somewhere in their history they decided they must be superior or die. The difficult work they face is learning to use their heart by releasing and removing all the walls they've created

---

*You can learn more about this in my book *Reweaving the Fabric of Your Reality*.

to keep themselves safe. They must learn to build a new connection of compassion through their heart.

In most cases, their heart has so many layers of protection that they do not even know its true nature. This becomes a daunting task. These individuals have been shamed and wounded so much that they confuse shame with guilt. Shame is believing you are bad; guilt is admitting you did a bad thing. Good people do bad things in third dimension. We all have committed acts where we felt shame. But having done something bad does not make you bad. The key to helping yourself in these situations is to find healers to help you quickly advance, learn meditation, and do it daily until you can move beyond your wounds.

The work of the MerKaBa meditation can make a huge difference. This is because the MerKaBa seals the heart in the fifth-dimensional field and prevents it from being wounded again. It allows you to be vulnerable without being exposed. In its original format, the 17-Breath MerKaBa meditation (MerKaBa Classic) takes you through a series of steps that allow you to activate an energy field around the body, which then allows you to access your fifth-dimensional self. It is an incredible practice that makes it easy to become fifth dimensional and stay there.* This is because it gives you access to energy fields that contain this vibration.

When you encounter a lower frequency from circumstances or individuals, you can maintain your higher vibration by choosing to love them anyway. This will allow you to coexist until they can meet you at your energy level. Then you will be able to view the opponent you see as your friend. If you are someone who is supporting others' transformation and they are manifesting their own drama—then love them anyway.

In fifth dimension you are expected to let your heart lead your

---

*Training in the MerKaBa Classic meditation is given on the DVD listed in Suggested Resources.

mind. Survival psychics use their higher chakra gifts to get information and control their environment and use this information with their minds. For them, it's about maintaining control. For them, it truly is a matter of life and death because somewhere in their history they decided they must win or they die. These people have a harder time healing their heart wounds, but it is possible. Because they are easily identified, as they seem tuned to higher realms yet act out in wounded ways, you can help by loving them anyway. As you become fifth-dimensional, you don't abandon your mind or your heart. As in ballroom dancing, there is one lead and one follower, yet they dance "as one." Your heart is the lead—the mind follows. This is a brand-new dance. This is your unique path into the fifth dimension. It has never been done this way before. You are on the cutting edge!

. . . .

**IN 5D, YOUR HEART IS THE LEAD—THE MIND FOLLOWS.
THIS IS A BRAND-NEW DANCE.**

. . . .

DEVELOPING TRUST

Trust is an important element of your new fifth-dimensional experience. You can begin to utilize it while still in third or fourth dimension. Consider a practice where you trust in a very proactive way. For example, when you stay at a hotel, do you bring your own preferred shampoo? Then do you need to take the free shampoo home? If not, then leave it behind. Trust that you have enough. When you are at a buffet restaurant, take smaller portions and trust there will be more food for you if you are still hungry. When waiting in line, encourage others who are seemingly in a big hurry to go ahead of you in a gracious and kind way. Once you personally adopt these practices, you will notice others do the same for you. You've changed your vibration, thus attracting more people like you, and have in fact increased the population of individuals acting the same way!

As my guides offered:

"We invite you to move into this level of concern for one another and trust. There is a difference between trust and knowing. Trust implies the possibility that you might fail. Knowing is certain belief that your success is all there is."

Trusting yourself may require a bigger effort. How will you know if it's okay to trust yourself or your intuition? Initially you won't. However, there are many ways to develop this trust factor so deeply that it transforms into knowing. One way is to keep a journal, noting every time you get some kind of knowing without knowing why or how you know. Decide to act on it, trusting it. Make note of these experiences in your calendar or journal. Over time this will develop into knowing.

Respecting yourself without coercion is also part of this trust. What will you do when no one is watching? Will you honor and respect others because it's the right thing to do? Recent research has shown that the people with good control over their thought processes, emotions, and behaviors not only flourish in school and in their jobs but are also healthier, wealthier, and more popular.[2]

What if you stop looking at what others are getting away with and instead decide to set the example, because it pleases you? Good leaders nurture others.

What ways could you find to respect and behave appropriately because you can and don't have to? What do you do when no one is watching? What if you decided to act as if respect toward yourself and others and all life was the only way to be? It isn't enough to "think" you are already doing this. Pay attention to those you love and admire. Their feedback will help you see your blind spots.

Trust implies that you could have a less desired outcome. What if you choose to break out of the mold/shell to become your true self? What if you didn't trust, but *knew* you could succeed? What would you do if you knew you could not fail?* Do you trust that the sun will rise every morning? Or do you know it? Knowing is certainty. The sun will rise. You cannot fail. Learn that trust is a choice to believe in yourself as much as God does. Would you doubt God? Why not adopt the attitude that you don't need to trust and that you just know?

This means you choose to check in with your Higher Self daily. Each day, choosing is part of your free will expression. Even the daily process of checking in with your Higher Self is an act of humility, as it doesn't use your will or ego to rely on previous information! The new trust produces a whole new economy, the sharing economy.

Could you allow a stranger in your home? Millions of people have, and they have met wonderful travelers. Look at the growth of such organizations as Airbnb, where members trust strangers in their homes. Trusting others with your home means that you know that you are part of a bigger whole and that everyone is connected. This sharing economy isn't just about homes or cars. Notice that many successful authors allow you to use their work as long as you give credit. I grant use of my work to anyone who asks, requesting a credit be given in exchange. We know and understand that we need each other to learn and grow; we benefit from sharing with each other.

. . . .

DECIDE YOU ALREADY KNOW THAT GOD BELIEVES IN YOU
AND YOU BELIEVE GOD. BECAUSE THIS IS THE FREE WILL ZONE,
EVERY DAY YOU RECEIVE A CLEAN SLATE. EVERY DAY YOU GET
TO CHOOSE. EVERY DAY YOU GET TO EXPLORE AND
DISCOVER WHAT YOU KNOW, AND WHAT YOUR
GUIDANCE TELLS YOU.

. . . .

---

*This question is often posited by Pat Bacilli, host of the talk radio show, *The Dr. Pat Show—Talk Radio to Thrive By.*

HOW DOES THIS COME TOGETHER?

This chapter may have challenged your belief systems. Decide to consider that there may be more possibilities in reality than you originally thought possible. Dissolving belief systems is part of waking up in 5D. You will not abandon beliefs—what you will do is expand your awareness, as this is how the mind works. You will magnify your comfort zone. Those who would hold you back prefer you remain in your current paradigm. Is your current belief system limited by the very narrow version of reality that you've endorsed and maintained here on Earth? As you expand and consider what is possible, more understanding becomes possible. Part of this engagement is the actual co-creation of a brand-new version of reality! It truly is both your training and your golden opportunity!

3
Ascension and the Five Dimensions

At this point in human history, everyone is getting the wake-up call. For some, they are magnetically drawn to challenge what they valued, along with their current choices. This spiritual awakening is part of the Great Shift that has been predicted for ages. It began with the so-called end of the Mayan calendar. Many teachers are calling it *Ascension*. Magically, I was asked to be part of the major ceremonies in Chichén Itzá for the end Mayan calendar. It's not the end of the line but a shift so great that it might seem to be. It is actually the beginning of amazing, powerful energy and frequencies that unhook us from our past patterns and make it easy for us to transform. Some of us are magnetically drawn to challenge what we valued, along with our current choices. Many of us have been waiting a long time for this! This big shift is the transformation of an age.

What have you been waiting for? Better understanding, clarity, sureness? There is no mistake. Understanding will come. Understanding will help you navigate through the amazing uplifting energy that is permeating you and everyone around you. This is your opportunity to educate yourself, become a master, and be part of the transformation of humanity. What an incredible opportunity! This chapter will give you overviews, and in later chapters we will dive deeper into this information.

WHAT IS ASCENSION?

Ascension is the dramatic physical, emotional, and spiritual transformation in humans that will cause you to feel, think, and be different than you were before. In the old days, we thought of Ascension in the Easter version, where Christ had to die to "ascend." This is not the case! This, in fact, is why this process is so mysterious. How could a person ascend and not die? Apart from the avatars and mystics, people have not ascended and maintained their physical body. It is largely unknown.

Does the Ascension mean you will die so that you can become enlightened or be reborn? No. Certainly not! Does this mean the end of 3D experiences and then going to the fourth dimension? No, and here's why. We are currently vacillating between fourth and fifth when we leave the third dimension. Right now, we are already moving toward our fifth-dimensional expression. Sometimes you are in 5D and don't even know it. That's why you need to wake up in 5D.

Why do we call it the Ascension if you are not going to die? It is because the transformation will make your "old" self literally unrecognizable. Just like the metamorphosis that occurs with all insects that pupate—bees, dragonflies, and butterflies—the transformation changes everything, yet the being remains alive. The Ascension of humanity on Earth is the perfected human's emergence from our current state of chrysalis; it is a foregone conclusion—inevitable. We are on our way but would benefit from some additional guidance. Like the caterpillar becoming the butterfly, the transformation is a mystery, but real. You may have heard of a science experiment where a caterpillar researcher provided too much outside intervention by attempting to help the caterpillar escape its cocoon. The result was misshapen wings! This is why self-education is so very important. In your case and for your own self-discovery, self-pace is critical to your success. It is for these reasons that you can and must assist your own process with your own efforts as an act of will. This is you stepping into your divinity. It is also you stepping into your fifth-dimensional self.

It's very unclear how each person will move into their fifth-dimensional expression. This is because you are living multiple realities and multiple versions of you. Your Ascension process is unique. As you become more conscious, daily choosing certain actions, behaviors, beliefs, and feelings that are based in the nonpolarity energy of unconditional acceptance, you begin to realize that you are in 5D far more than you thought. The multiple realities are collapsing into one.

Humanity is awakening to our new now. Your ego and mind developed skills that were needed and used for physical presence. This you have mastered. Now you are ready for the next evolution. New codes in you are being activated. The next "wave" of evolution is now upon you. This is your opportunity to bring higher consciousness into everything. Just like you might bring a dish to share at a family event, what if you chose to bring your highly evolved consciousness as a gift, reminding yourself you are in service to (not better than) those at this family event? You can be part of your own healing and that of others. You can contribute positively to humanity's transformation by being yourself in 5D. Many skills will come easily to you in 5D that were seemingly unreachable in 3D.

As you ultimately become more and more fifth-dimensional, you become the Ascended Master yourself! Your own process is unique and will not move faster than you will allow. For some, your shift in consciousness will seem radical to your friends. For others, it will be such a gradual but clear "awakening" that its expression will seem smooth. For sure, everyone who desires this is becoming an Ascended Master. As you grow and develop your unique expression of you as an Ascended Master who is your fifth-dimensional expression, your Ascension will bring change upon the Earth. Mother Earth will not "ascend without you." This is why all of heaven (and earth) is waiting, watching and—as in the lyrics from the famous John Lennon song, *Imagine*—the world will "live as one."

Physical

The ascended body is the same as your fifth-dimensional body, which will be more full of light: slightly translucent and quite possibly aglow.

Many of you have seen this version of you or other beings in your meditations and did not realize this is where everyone is going! For sure, there are those who will dig in their heels, and say, "I like this [old] version of reality just fine." They will be given every opportunity to understand that the world as they know it is coming to an end. They will not be able to sustain it and the choices will be to join the New Earth or perish with the old one! So how will you use this information? How will you become fifth dimensional?

Because the Ascension is physical for the first time, there's much to be learned and discovered. Many people will experience physical discomfort. The more you resist, the more challenging these changes can become. You might have made multiple visits to various doctors, yet no one can find any reason for your physical pain and discomfort! And of course, this can cause even more distress. If this describes you, after you have exhausted all the traditional sources of healers, you may want to explore nontraditional healers. You may discover that craniosacral therapy, acupuncture, naturopathy, meditation, and a whole host of other tools may help you get through your personal physical shift. You may also find a shift in your diet will help.

Experiences can crop up that are actually clearing past life wounds. What if some of what you may be physically healing from comes from other lifetimes or other timelines? What if you are merging other versions of you that are damaged? It's important to consider this because, as you open to these possibilities, the energies can merge with who you are much easier! Once you start to look with clear intention, you'll be led to the individuals ideally suited to help you! You'll also grow your Higher Self connection.

Emotional

Emotions are one of your portals. Keep yourself in peace and emotional balance. Even when doing so, you may find your emotions are all over the map! Emotional trauma may be at the source of your awakening. This is true for many. This is so important that I have devoted a full chapter to exploring this deeply (chapter 5). Emotions are distinctly human; emotion is the ability to imbue *chi* (energy that has no charge) with a purpose. The purpose is to express a feeling. Feelings are meant to be expressed. Feelings are as important as experiences; they steer our experiences and give them more depth. Most women develop awareness of feelings, while most men focus on experiences. A balanced human equally experiences both. As you become aware of who you are, as a male or female, you will discover whatever you've chosen to emphasize, and you will be drawn to develop the other side.

The Interplay of Thoughts, Feelings, and Actions in Fifth Dimension

Be in the moment—yet sensitive to the wind.

Learn about your environment, but don't let it rule you.

Learn to understand your feelings and trust them.

Think before you act translates now into think and feel before you act.

Think before you act translates into look both ways and then up to your 5D self before taking action!

Be fearless (not reckless). You can foster this by making a list of your fears and then asking them to tell you what they are about.

In fifth dimension, fears no longer rule you.

Mental

The mind has ruled for a long time. There are lots of good reasons for this. Western society has long held that logic is the only reasonable form of arriving at conclusions. This is especially true in the sciences. We are slowly beginning to unlock the mind's stronghold on thought processes. Logic is based on repeatable, verifiable systems. Doesn't that make it a form of prediction? Isn't it interesting that most of the world's major mathematical and scientific breakthroughs have occurred not from mental posturing but from meditation or intuition? Most breakthroughs have come as a result of some mystical experience! The ego wants to cling to the old patterns because it's the ego's job to keep you safe. Fear of the unknown is often the root of mental and emotional drama. Where does the ego get its determination of what is safe for you? It comes from your history. This is why learning to step out of patterns and confidently asking, "What's going on?" becomes so very critical. It opens the way to learn, accept, and adopt something you did not know or understand from your experiences or feelings!

Spiritual

The spiritual shift is driving all of humanity upward. In the process of Ascension, or waking up in 5D, your inner motives will change. Many individuals here have already achieved Ascension and are now here as way-showers. Way-showers don't need to prove anything. Their purpose comes from within. It's based on deep service to humanity and deep love for all living things. Many of the things that will happen to you are transcendent. You may start seeing auras or know things about people. Perhaps you will start feeling strong urges that you are to do more than just work at a corporate job. Because of the light activating your new expression, anything that is not in alignment with these new energies will become uncomfortable. You may think you need these things, but the longer you hold out, the more dramatic your shift. Cling to them if you must and let go as soon as you can. Your well-being depends on it. Your entire consciousness is pulling you toward your Higher Self expression.

HOW DO YOU KNOW IF
YOU ARE IN FIFTH DIMENSION?

In fifth dimension you don't really care about anything, including yourself. It's not apathy; it's a level of compassion that requires nothing from you yet allows you to be present and loving toward everything. You are clear that your needs will be met with grace and ease, and you don't need to take sides or race to get ahead of someone else! This is one of the many ironies of the fifth dimension compared to third. You don't care if people don't like you, and you don't care if you are different. You do have compassion. You do care about people, but not to the point that it holds you back or locks you into something that isn't a fit for you.

You know you are in fifth dimension because you are honest and kind and it's easy to be honest in a kindhearted way. You don't hide little things or big things to protect yourself or someone else. You find it easy to feel compassion for yourself and others. You admit your mistakes since, yes, you can still inadvertently hurt someone. You see the humor in difficult situations. You may even notice you're responding with kindness and empathy toward others, even when you weren't expecting or planning to do so.

How can you tell if other people are in fifth dimension? They will be fun, funny, irreverent, joyful, loving, and peaceful. You will be able to tell because they understand (everything) and are pleasant even when things go awry. They are patient and kind. They can still have a standard and be firm but never angry or hurtful.

Now that you have some idea of events to come, let's look at what exactly is going on when you wake up in fifth dimension. Your abilities will be expanded and deepened. You'll have different needs, different food preferences, and different desires. You might find your sleep patterns are disrupted. You may be surprised when you aren't attracted to certain types of food anymore. You may discover that certain pastimes no longer interest you.

In fact, you may have even chosen to be born into a family where you don't feel you belong. If you feel this way, then you probably don't belong! Why would you choose that? It is a way for you to learn first-hand the ways of Earth so you are well prepared to serve humanity as you discover your true roots. Not being "from here" usually means you are part of the more evolved, spiritually focused society emerging in fifth dimension.

This book is about being proactive. How can you actively use the thrust of 5D energy to support you? Before we get into that, let's get clarity on the first through fourth dimensions.

THE FIRST THROUGH FOURTH DIMENSIONS

The dimensions are so vast that our ability to conceive of and comprehend them is limited by our perceptions. Even though I have endeavored to outline the dimensions here, please understand that there are overtone series that provide for multiple variations of the dimensions. The multiples are almost limitless. The overtone principle is based on music and physics. A way to understand this is to think of a stringed instrument: When one of the strings is plucked, it vibrates at the full length, producing a specific pitch; the first overtone is produced where the string naturally vibrates at the halfway mark. The next division is half again or one-fourth, and these notes become the next overtone series since there will be more than one. It is possible to continue this subdivision endlessly. Similarly, right now, there are multiple versions of this reality. Within this system there are groups and subgroups converging in multiple timelines. Ideally humanity will wind its way back to one. This is more tangible in the 3D world than in the higher realms. As we shift our perceptions from what is probable to what is possible, our vision too will expand to receive it. Here is a partial list of dimensions most people are currently experiencing, along with their qualities (see table 3.1 on page 56).

First Dimension

First dimension is inner focused, and it's all about the single point. It is an awareness of self-awareness. It can be expressed as a single tone. This is why a practice such as toning is so powerful, because it fixes anything that is broken at first dimension. Toning is using the voice to create a sound. It can be based on a vowel to start, such as "Ohhhh." If you want, you can then add a consonant, such as toning "Om," but the consonant is not required. Toning is like singing except that you

TABLE 3.1. DIMENSIONS AND QUALITIES

Dimension	Awareness	Location in Reality	Movement	What You Notice
First Dimension	Self-awareness	Inside third	None	Existence
Second Dimension	Point (self) and line (other)	Inside third	None	Relationship; beginning of contrast; Self/other
Third Dimension	Time and space; physical, mental, emotional, and etheric bodies	Here!	Linear	Cause and effect
Fourth Dimension	Vortex energy	Astral plane	Emotion-based, higher intensity	Whirlwind: pulling up; quicksand: pulling down
Fifth Dimension	Peaceful, knowing, joyful	Our new now!	Multi-directional	Thoughts, speech, and action all are in alignment; anything that is out of integrity is painful

do not need words, only vowels. When you are willing to make sounds in a playful way, as you might in the shower, you are far more likely to fill your voice with the vibration of what you really need. I encourage you to do this all the time, any time that you can. When you are stuck in your car by yourself or in the shower are great places to start. When you feel confident, you might share this with any groups you meet with to study, learn, or meditate. Do your toning first, and watch how your meditations improve. Allow toning to occur in free form. This is the energy of the will of God. Imagine if you are God: you already know everything; there is nothing to know. Isn't this what God is?

Why would we come into embodiment and experience all that we experience? We chose to separate from that which is inseparable. We chose to create a veil that allows us to experience the not-God choice. We desired to experience more than what we had, when we had everything. It comes from self-awareness. Was this wanting more greedy? If you are an artist, and you feel like you have explored everything you want to explore and want to move into another medium, does someone look at you and say, "What's wrong with you? Why don't you stick with watercolor?" Of course they do not say that. Your feeling is an expansion, an expansion of the database.

In the process of coming from the all-knowing, we separated from that which is inseparable. It is as though we created a veil, pretending that we are not God or acting as if we don't have resources. This is like the prince who goes into the streets to experience what it would be like to be poor. Why would we do that? We incarnate to increase that which would not be increased any other way.

Second Dimension

The second dimension is "outer focused." In it we work with the wisdom of God. Its musical expression is the monochromatic scale. Think of a piano keyboard; in that scale is every single key. Whether black or white, each key is part of the scale. In this kind of scale, the pitches are very close. It's based on a point and line and can be imagined by thinking of a single piece of paper. There is no depth, but there is length and width. In a meditation in one of my classes, a student asked to go back to his first expression in creation. He saw himself as being like a flat piece of paper! Perhaps it was something like how the cartoon of the Queen of Hearts playing card in the Disney movie *Alice in Wonderland* walks like a flat piece of paper, without depth. Second dimension has a limitation that is answered by 3D.

Third Dimension

The third dimension is a projection from other dimensions, just like movies are a series of stills, shown in a way that makes the mind expand them into movement. This 3D field is based on numbers and relationship; we have both the linear awareness of step-by-step-by-step processes and relationships between people, places, and things. This ability to experience contrast gives all kinds of relationships to anything that we create. Once you are in 5D it becomes obvious that you've been projecting from other dimensions.

Many highly evolved people who have come to the planet at this time experience disgust, concern, sadness, and more at the sorry state of affairs they discover here. For them, the desire to escape and go back to God is sometimes overwhelming. If this describes you, if you have this desire (for escape) you are here to assist the transition of the planet. Your discomfort serves as a driving force to help the world. Many of you incarnate into difficult situations to stop the drama. Many of you have been told by my guides that the abuse stopped with you. It usually means Earth is not your true home, and along with this comes the desire to "go home." That desire is normal, but if this is you and you long to "go home," it may also mean that you are not doing your work. It's hard. Darn. All you have to do is step up to your work (your mission), and that desire vanishes.

Why do you feel this way? Because you are so plugged into God that being here (existing) is physically painful. The antidote to that pain is to do your work, serving others in some way. By the way, we are not talking servitude here but service. Your discomfort stems from either not doing your mission or *believing* you cannot do your mission. Maybe you've not figured that out yet, but that's how it shows up. If this is you, try this simple prayer,

Dear God, show me how much I am loved. Help me to find and complete my mission.

The goal here is to work toward balance of relationships, and the things that we interact with, the structures. Third dimension is based in physical matter, but inner focused. This is you, a spiritual energy, becoming physical, and experiencing that!

Higher-dimensional individuals have important awareness. This is why some of you may find it physically painful to be around certain situations, people, and so on. You must limit anything that drives your energy to a place of discomfort. Pay attention if you are in a place where you are exposed to disturbing sounds or images, such as seeing a violent film in a movie theater (leave). Once you achieve mastery, it won't matter, as you can tune it out. Until then, don't be afraid to walk out of a room or place that just doesn't feel good to you! This reinforces who you really are.

On the other hand, some people have so much angelic energy that all they have to do is be here. Many a client has been told by his or her record keepers, "Your job is to hold the God Consciousness on the planet in the purest possible way. You must give yourself permission to avoid experiences that cause you pain." You have to be very selective about what you let into your life. If your good friends use swear words, ask them to stop—or get new friends. Remind them gently; tell them it's painful for you to hear. If you are in an abusive job or relationship, ask your angels and guides to help you solve this. Maybe you will get a better job or maybe that offensive person will leave. Ask for a miracle, and then demand a miracle! What about external influences? Do you need a TV? Over forty years ago my first TV broke, and I didn't replace it. A surprise outcome was that one of my sons, who was dyslexic, started to read! Today he's an engineer.

Fourth Dimension

Fourth dimension still carries polarity, and as such has a high and low area. There is a faster moving energy here, which I've seen as quicksand, as the vortex energy that pulls you downward, sometimes below third dimension. The upward movement feels like a soft tornado—gently lifting you into higher realms. Fourth dimension also holds the energy known as the astral plane. This is an area within the lower fourth dimension where many of the demons, entities, and other unsavory energies reside. Finally, fourth dimension is a place of emotions and their expression. It is also a highly creative zone but still expresses polarity. There is no real need to "go" to fourth dimension. You instinctively use the fourth dimension as a portal or nexus point. Many move through it quickly; it is the zone of transition. It is not a location you arrive at purposefully. Nor is it where you want to go and stay, but ideally it is how you get to where you are going. Consider it as the hub between third and fifth.

Fourth dimension is the place where you often find you are experiencing deep emotions. Both deep happiness and sadness can be found in the fourth dimension. The deep sadness can pull you down like quicksand. Great joy can spiral you upward to fifth dimension. It's generally not noticeable to you unless the emotion is intense. Maybe someone important to you is leaving you. Maybe you've had an experience of intense emotion because someone died; yet it's also where something spiritual happened to you. You haven't been able to re-create it—and it changed you. Maybe it gave you an insight, or gave you wisdom, compassion, or self-mastery.

Typically, the fourth dimension doesn't really seem that much different from third dimension. You might not notice you've moved into fourth dimension. Very often, coming through fourth dimension isn't realized until you are back in 3D and you notice something unusual happening. Fourth dimension is a highly creative place, yet not productive. One marker of being in fourth dimension is the escalated emotions. Another marker is disappearing items.

Have you ever had something disappear and you search for it high and low—even the last place you were sure that it was left? Some time later, after you've emptied your purse or a drawer, it turns up exactly where you were sure you left it? Originally when this would happen to me, I asked, "Where did my stuff go?" My Higher Self would always provide the answer—"It's in the fourth dimension." It was not until I asked, "What's going on?" that I discovered I had been in the fourth dimension when I set it down—and when I was back in third, the item wasn't visible! Once I understood this, I could easily retrieve things by saying, "If my missing item is in the fourth dimension—I'd like it back. Thank you." Then it would turn up exactly where I had been looking before. You are also experiencing the shifting between dimensions if your "stuff" is disappearing, and you can get your missing stuff back in the same way, by asking, "I'd like my [name it] back." Then you will shift back into that higher frequency, and voilà, your missing items will be exactly where you left them!

The reason this solution statement works is that you have moved out of the emotion of *anxiousness* and into a state of *acceptance*. It might be the first level of acceptance, but it gets you started, moves you out of negative emotion, and increases the likelihood of your shifting into a higher dimension long enough to locate the missing item. The fourth dimension, even though it seems the same as or similar to third dimension, is a vibrational level that you project that allows you to simultaneously see and do things in both fourth and third. Yet when you are only vibrating in third dimension, a fourth-dimensional action doesn't show up. These experiences are what led me to understand the nature of expanding consciousness and expressions in the higher dimensions.

Fourth dimension is meant to create movement—to push you higher or lower. It allows you to move into a very fluid location that carries with it vibrations in either direction. The portal itself doesn't serve to transform you. Instead, your shift into intense emotion causes you to *become* fourth dimensional. You might pass through it quickly if you are heart-centered and focused. The energy of the portal is you moving lower or higher. Imagine standing at the base of an escalator. It will not take you higher until you step onto it! Have you ever experienced the feeling of your emotions getting the better of you? Have you ever felt emotionally out of control? Have you ever known you were spiraling down yet were unable or unwilling to stop it? All of these are expressions of fourth dimension moving downward. In the lower section of fourth dimension you'll encounter dark energies. Which direction will you choose? Will you use the portal to ease into a higher energy?

The transition zone between the third and fifth is weighted in your favor. All of heaven has made the higher expressions of emotions in fourth dimension inviting, energizing, and attractive. In this energy you will become more aware via inklings. Pay attention to them and honor them, as each inkling or insight that you honor and use will proactively lead you to even more awareness. This honest awareness of what you might choose next will allow you to make choices that help you shift and evolve rapidly upward, sometimes allowing you to slip right into fifth dimension without even noticing.

....

ALL OF HEAVEN HAS MADE THE HIGHER EXPRESSIONS OF EMOTIONS IN FOURTH DIMENSION INVITING, ENERGIZING, AND ATTRACTIVE. IN THIS ENERGY YOU WILL BECOME MORE AWARE VIA INKLINGS. PAY ATTENTION TO THEM AND HONOR THEM, AS EACH INKLING OR INSIGHT THAT YOU HONOR AND USE WILL PROACTIVELY LEAD YOU TO EVEN MORE AWARENESS.

....

Fifth Dimension

Fifth dimension will put you in the tranquil zone. How can you go from fourth to fifth? This can occur when you completely line up (resonate) your emotional body with your physical body. The way this is done is to project yourself into a wormhole, which functions something like a combination lock, in which all the layers line up. It is when your physical, mental, and emotional aspects line up and match. You can accomplish this in several ways.

The easiest way is to start with a clear intention and then work it out from there. Begin with a visual or an intention that clearly shows the results of being fifth dimensional in a 3D body. Your first objective is to make sure there is no conflict between your thoughts and emotions or with your emotions and your actions. True integrity is at the core of remaining fifth dimensional. When you think one thing, act another, and feel yet another, you have created a roadblock to being fifth dimensional. How many times have you caught yourself in denial about something? That's when you'll find out you are out of sync with yourself and cannot maintain fifth dimension.

Notice what resistance you have in your body. Notice what resistance you have in your mind. Notice the resistance in your heart. Invite the resistance to be released. Sometimes it is released through movement, dance, chiropractic adjustments, and, ideally, somatics. Somatics is a technique created by Thomas Hanna, Ph.D. It can be a hands-on system of stretches that free the body's resistance with the approach to renewed control of the muscles through use of the voluntary motor system. Resistance is sometimes released through exercise (qigong is spectacular).

You may have been taught to think and believe life is a struggle, yet it is not! Keep a gratitude journal, thank God for everything, and you will find that everything is solved easily and dissolved easily. Don't get attached to the drama. Don't get lost in your emotional experiences; use them to bridge you to higher consciousness as they were meant to do. Buddhists say, "Your thoughts are not you." Equally so, your emotions are not you!

Begin to see the humor in everything. If people say you laugh a lot, thank them. If you laugh even about the tough things, then you are probably already being fifth dimensional at least some of the time. As you move toward upper fourth dimension, you no longer experience affront. Imagine not even noticing an insult coming your way. Here's an example of when that once happened to me. I had planned to be with my mother on the first anniversary of my sister's death, knowing how hard it would be for her. I went to church with her and my stepfather, and we had just emerged from the church service. In that moment of her grief I was in deep gratitude for being able to be there for her. My mother was driving, and my stepfather wanted me to sit in the front seat, something I had never done while traveling in the car with them. I politely refused, suggesting he sit there. After I finally got in the front seat, at his insistence, he accused me of "being just like my mother." I actually heard only the compliment! I turned to him. "Thank you; that is one of the nicest things you've ever said to me." It wasn't sarcastic or angry. It was peaceful.

As someone who is blonde, I've often joked that "you cannot insult a blonde. Why? Because she only hears compliments!" That's another mark of being in fifth dimension—everything is funny. Deepak Chopra's book *Why Is God Laughing?* is aptly titled.

The Nurturing Response

The nurturing response is a prime directive that humanity can immediately shift to help people stay anchored in 5D. So when anything happens, the first action of the person who has not been affected is, "Are you okay?" This is common to a mother, when her child falls. She asks, "Are you okay?" Yet many people have not been nurtured and have such holes in their hearts that they don't even know what that means. So we give you the precise example. The next step is to explore why or how. But the first step is the nurturing response. Train yourself. When anything disruptive happens, if you are the one left standing, you must say, "Are you okay?" and then ask, "What's going on? Who did this? Why did this happen?" But only after you determine that everyone is okay.

Sometimes you are put in such a difficult situation that you are super frustrated. You cannot seem to reason or work with someone. Consider the nurturing response. How do you choose the nurturing response? When you start to experience an affront, take a breath and a pause! Ask for help from your angels and guides. Recognize that sometimes the other party isn't trying to upset you; instead he is simply trying to express his feelings or his wound! For your part, you see it as a call for help, which arouses your nurturing response. Ask for help in developing your own nurturing response. Clearing intention each day during your daily meditations will help you land in 5D!

The nurturing response acknowledges the other's pain. What if you really did hurt someone's feelings and she is reacting to you? It's appropriate then to announce, "I had no idea I did that." Even if it's painful for you to admit that you might have harmed someone, it's important to acknowledge his or her pain. This transforms everyone involved. Gratitude is key. You may have been taught that anger is justified. It is never justified. Whenever I encounter fierce anger or this type of energy the answer is always the same: practice the nurturing response. Practice Ho'oponopono. It is an incredibly powerful tool to help you step out of ego-based thought action or reaction and step into fifth dimension.

Relationships in 5D

Relationships provide one of the fastest opportunities to manifest your 5D self, maintain safety, and create more 5D experiences. Let us explore how this works. In 3D when someone hurts you physically or hurts your feelings, very likely causing some sort of pain, you want an apology. You may feel you're entitled to one. These are wonderful concepts in 3D. However in 5D it doesn't work that way at all.

At 5D you can still be disappointed. Yet you don't need an apology. This is because there is no judgment! Remember, an apology implies the other person is bad or wrong. Instead you want to receive comfort from the other person. Your family, friends, or beloved, or the person who has the biggest influence, who is closest to you, can give you comfort and appreciation for the experience. And that lets you release the feelings instantly. We've all been around a little child who comes running to you with a raised injured finger saying how much it hurts because it just got caught in a door. And if you nurture him right away, he will stop crying, squirm, and be done with drama quickly. If, however, you choose to dismiss his situation, "Go back outside and play; there's nothing wrong with your finger," or say to him, "I know that door is broken, and I need to fix that; I'll get to it later this week," you're completely ignoring him and validating yourself.

While it is important to validate yourself first, you need to be doing that work on your own—on your own time—so that you can be of service when your family member or partner is in pain and needs comfort. Remember, the heart leads and the mind follows. The ego rules at 3D, which means all you care about is saving face: "Who is to blame?" At 5D, the heart loves, and all you care about is comforting someone in his or her pain.

Each gender has its own preferred way of operating. Men are very action oriented; women are more likely to be speech oriented. So when a woman needs comforting, the man can reach over and hug her. That's his action. When a woman is doing the comforting, she might say, "Are you okay?" Women give grace, and men give comfort.

When my husband does something that causes me pain, I don't want an apology. An apology implies that I have a standard he's missing that makes me better than him. Desiring or expecting an apology is a form of imposing my version of reality upon him. That would lock me into 3D. I don't judge my husband. I can be hurt when I've depended on him for something and it doesn't work out. While it's important for me that he hears my feeling, it is not important for me to get an apology. I believe that once he realizes how I feel, it will suffice to guide him to behave in a different way in the future. On other hand, if he can offer comfort and acknowledge my pain without claiming blame, that opens the hearts of both. Acknowledgment says, "Oh my gosh, I know you were hurt." It does not take up the source of the hurt but instead validates it. Validation of experience is the God response. It acknowledges the experience occurred without requiring the person to bend the knee or be the "responsible party."

When my children were younger they were required to fold their own clothes after washing and drying them. From about age eight onward, my children wore wrinkled clothes! This was uncomfortable for me. I wanted them to look their best because I like to look my best. But I felt that if they didn't want to fold their clothes and were content to pull wrinkled clothes out of the clean laundry basket, then I should let them be. I kept hoping that peer pressure would kick in and they would decide to either fold their clothes in a timely manner or iron them. What happened instead was completely innovative. They came home with a laundry product, a spray that allowed them to smooth out the wrinkles almost instantly. This is very exciting. Nonjudgment will open the way to all kinds of new solutions.

We've taught our children that an apology is due or a debt is owed when a mistake is made. In 3D when something goes wrong we have an injury and then expect an apology. If something is broken, restitution is made. We have right and wrong; we have a victim and a perpetrator. In 5D we can have injury and acknowledgment, acceptance and comfort; the absence of judgment produces expansion of love in both. The Course in Miracles teaches apology is not necessary because there are no affronts.

TABLE 3.2. SOMETHING GOES "WRONG"

These reactions keep you locked in 3D	These reactions anchor you in 5D
Injury leading to apology	Injury leading to comfort
Hurt leading to restitution	Acceptance
Right vs. wrong	Acknowledgment
Victim vs. perpetrator	Nonjudgment
	Result: love expands!

VERY REAL EXPERIENCES GOING FROM 3D INTO 5D

In 5D you can even change reality as it stands. One of the most important tools you can use is my personal request of the universe: *I am asking for a day of Heaven on Earth.* When you make this invocation you change the reality. How? You have given yourself and anyone you meet the energy imprint of 5D, Heaven on Earth.

In one very specific instance I gave this invocation in the morning ceremony of a workshop. While in meditation earlier that morning, my host Eliona, a nurse, observed a car accident outside her house at the busy corner intersection where she and her family lived. Later that morning, when she heard tires screeching and the sound of a car crash, she went running out to the street. Without thinking, she asked the men, who were standing outside their damaged cars, "Where's the woman?" She was asking about the woman she had seen in her meditation that morning who had been badly injured and in need of serious medical attention. The men, still in a bit of a daze, answered her, "Oh, at the last minute she decided not to come." When Eliona came back into the class she asked how she could have seen one thing in her meditation and yet another later? I reminded her that we had asked for "A Day of Heaven on Earth for ourselves and everyone we come in contact with." My guides declared that our prayer in the opening ceremony changed the reality to a fifth-dimensional version, where the woman did not have to go through the experience of the accident!

What to Do if It Is You

If you are about to be in an auto accident and there is nothing you can do, "close your eyes." Closing your eyes is a way to move into fifth dimension and pass through the accident. You can say "peace," "safety," or any words that make it easy for you to be centered and in your heart to produce results that defy expectation.

"Impossible" Safety

So many instances of movement from 3D to 5D in relation to accidents have been reported to me that I quit keeping track. Originally, I intended to write a book just about this single category! Ken Page reported driving down the freeway and coming up to a major traffic accident involving a tractor-trailer rig and multiple cars. As he tells it, he looked at a crystal he was holding and the next thing he knew, he could see the pileup of cars in his rearview mirror and the path in front of him was free and clear. I read a sweet book published by Hallmark Cards that also reported a similar incident, where a woman observed a car that pulled out of a driveway in a blinding snowstorm, right into the path of an oncoming semi-tractor-trailer rig—yet there was no harm. The car emerged completely intact! In yet another example, Jeff Pelez, a student from a class in Sarasota, reported a similar "impossible non-accident," which defied all known laws of physics. In his story Jeff was driving into a blind curve. There was a large fence on the other side, so there was no way a car could pass. Yet there was a yellow car behind him that was trying to go around his car. He moved into the opposite lane, when a third (red) car in the opposing lane suddenly appeared facing him. There was no way the yellow car trying to pass him could have gone around. Yet moments later the red car he had been facing (for a certain collision) was now behind him!

A friend's daughter was driving up a steep hill in Los Angeles. It was rush hour, and her car was in the far left lane when her engine failed! She closed her eyes and thought only the word "safe." When she opened her eyes next, she could "see" her deceased grandmother sitting next to her. She was also on the shoulder at the far right side of the road and was able to get help.

In yet one more story, my friend Carol Kakoczky was driving her brand-new car when she saw a young woman driving a car that was headed right into her car. It hit her car split seconds later. Her thought just before the collision was, "Be safe!" She kept reciting this, over and over, like a mantra. "Be safe." The other car spun around after hitting Carol's car, narrowly missed a tractor trailer, rolled several times, and then finally came to a stop across the freeway. The semi-truck driver was so stunned he pulled over (maybe she did pass through him), and the woman got out of her car with no injuries!

The Surprising Ease of Sliding Back and Forth

One of the surprising things to people who are still thinking in a 3D way is that it is possible to slide from third dimension into fourth or fifth and back to third without noticing or even understanding that it has occurred. It is only in hindsight that you begin to use perspective to notice what has happened. You may start to notice you are "going fifth dimensional" because you are feeling blissful and loving in a difficult situation. It may mean you will know what is happening around you before others realize it. It might give you the ability to stay heart centered, patient, and loving in spite of challenging circumstances.

Please note, when you are actually in 5D you do not see the situation's challenge—it is only when you slip back into 3D and think about it that it begins to dawn on you and you realize that you have avoided certain disaster and how different you were in those 5D moments. This is the beginning of going 5D.

After completion of a MerKaBa meditation class with me, Kelley shared the following experience:

"My husband and I recently traveled to another state to attend our son's police graduation ceremony. I really don't like to travel to this location because of how dense and heavy the energy feels to me in that area. In the days leading up to the trip, I had been receiving messages that we would also be doing some work in anchoring in some higher frequencies while we were there.*

"I also received the message that this might knock me out of the blissful vibration I had been holding for the last few weeks. But of course, when you're feeling so good, you're thinking, 'There's no way that's going to happen!' Well, as a lot of us know, the work of transmuting lower energies and anchoring in higher ones can many times take its toll energetically, and nearly boot you back to the same old third dimension energies. I also received the message that I might discover some new tools as a result of this trip (that message should have been my first clue this might not be pleasant)!† During my son's induction ceremony, I was caught off guard when a disturbing video was shown unexpectedly. It was quite upsetting."

When Kelley and I spoke about her experience, I described her reaction to the unexpected video like this:

"Very sensitive people [such as Kelley and me] can be knocked way out by objectionable experiences. In other words, there are certain persons on the planet who are actively holding the higher frequencies for everyone else. When they encounter any kind of violence or disturbing

---

*More details can be found on our joint blog post at www.Kelleyknight.com/blog.
†When Kelley says "not pleasant," she is comparing what it feels like to be in her fifth-dimensional state to then temporarily sliding out of it.

lower vibrational energies, it can make them feel like they have lost their connection to the Divine. And in fact, that is exactly what has happened. When you are fifth dimensional, you are plugged into the Divine.

"When we're really tuned in and connected to our Higher Self, we experience everything as real, and we don't have time to suspend disbelief like we automatically do when going to see a movie at the theater. Most people have such heavy filters in place that they don't notice or have this type of reaction.

"As a person becomes more fifth dimensional, purity replaces these filters and challenging or difficult visuals are physically painful, because they are not expressing unconditional love. At some point, when all of humanity is vibrating at this level, this will no longer be an issue."

Kelley continues:

"After being home a few days from the trip and still feeling like I'd been hit by an energetic freight train, I decided that beginning the next day I was going back to fifth dimension no matter what!"

Stating out loud that she wanted to be "back in" fifth dimension where she'd been hanging out since the completion of the MerKaBa class helped Kelley to start on her way back "up"; her intention/desire to return to that frequency provided her with tools to do just that. Once you've been there, you can always find your way back.

Kelley reflected:

"We may find that easier said than done, but that's where Maureen and her theory of resonance in physics and a couple cool new tools come in!"

One of the things that Kelley did for herself was to call me some days later. During her conversation with me, she mentioned multiple times that she could feel her frequency rising. This happens when two sources, both vibrating at different frequencies, one faster/higher and the other slower/lower, come into resonance. The higher frequency is used as a focal point, which draws the lower into resonance with it. In Kelley's case her strong desire to rise and match the faster/higher frequency made it possible.

First was her act of will. She decided that she was not participating in the lower energy any longer. It was not her truth; therefore it was not her reality. She felt an immediate shift.

Next, her Higher Self and the universe provided a situation (connecting with me) that also would enable her to raise her personal vibration, and that was enough to put her right back into fifth dimension. She says, "It happened with a resounding *thump*!"

About the thump—it wasn't a smooth landing. After our long conversation, she was fine and felt really good! Yet within fifteen minutes things deteriorated rapidly. Her stomach began to feel as if it were in a Vise-Grip, and then she began to feel extremely nauseous! She asked her Higher Self and received information that it was energetic, and not physical illness. However, for her, it was manifesting itself physically, big time!! She was doing everything she could do to minimize it. This included Lamaze breathing techniques used during childbirth and anything she could to avoid getting sick!

Next she felt the odd urge to be in water! I had also suggested she take an Epsom salts bath to clear her energy. She didn't have any on hand so she decided the water in the shower would have to be enough to wash away any energetic debris.

Kelley relates:

"As soon as I was out of the water, I had this amazing openness, with information pouring in, and it just kept increasing! I was getting the answer to anything I could possibly think of, before I could even finish thinking of it!! I knew I was totally back in fifth dimension!

"Then, I got the full download of what had taken place. . . . I had been asking for this, remember? I decided that on the next day I was going to be at least fifth dimension again. It was such a strong intention that the universe provided a 'tool,' that is, connecting with Maureen who holds this energy, to assist me in clearing the last of whatever it was that put me back where I was before the trip, which is what I had very strongly asked for.

"In addition, I realized that the fast boost to my energy system, changing vibration and frequency so quickly (not to mention dimensions), was what was giving me the physical symptoms. So then I finally remembered the new tool I had gotten a day earlier when I decided I would no longer participate in the lower energy and made the intention/decision/choice that I would wake up the next day in fifth dimension. So I said, 'I choose to experience this reboot with no ill effects to my physical body.' And it let up, a lot! Not all the way, but enough to where I could stop the Lamaze breathing!"

Kelley makes an important point—that when we choose to return quickly to the fifth dimension, it's advisable to add "in grace and ease!"

There are so many factors impacting your ability to stay in 5D that it can be overwhelming. What will you do about it? Ultimately it is an act of will. Anybody who gets knocked out of 5D and then decides to change his or her vibration will attract what is needed to make that happen. Kelley is a highly evolved and spiritually developed individual who is so ready to practice this information. You can too.

THOSE WHO CAN'T HOLD YOU BACK

We are in the last phase of "those who would hold humanity back" energy. I am not attempting to address that problem. I'm simply identifying the very real fact that there is a power and force whose agenda is to hold back humans from their Ascension, from becoming fifth-dimensional God-selves. As I mentioned in the previous chapter, humanity has been "held back" by energies and beings that have a vested interest in humans remaining locked in the concept that it is not possible to change or improve our lives.

Reading this is one key to your transformation. Reread this if you don't understand. Then go back to the previous chapter, where I describe how your Ascension is now guaranteed. They cannot hold you back any longer. You have considerably more power and resources than you can even suspect. The key is your imagination.

4

Tools for 5D Living and Signs You're There

In this chapter we will begin to explore tools you can use to set the stage for waking up in 5D and the basic awareness of your fifth-dimensional self, as well as some of the signs and symptoms of being in fifth dimension.

The first and most important thing is clear intention. You can start the process with a simple prayer when you go to sleep at night—*I ask that I wake up in 5D*. As mentioned earlier, I began calling in fifth dimensional energies when I started teaching others to ask for "a day of Heaven on Earth for me and everyone I come in contact with." This produces magical results. As I write this I am also hearing, "and especially for anyone I am in contract with!"

You can consciously tap in to this energy by making clear intention. Because you have a clean slate every day, you get to decide what intention to set each day. You get to decide to be full of love for life, for your fellow human, for yourself, and all living things on the Earth! Imagine you are on one of those transponders from *Star Trek*. Imagine that your destination is set. That's you deciding to be 5D. This makes it easy for you to be where you need to be to produce what you need to produce. Where you focus your energy and where you put your awareness *is* your location.

Quantum physics offers us some clarification about this, explaining that even when particle and wave are being measured, evidence is there to prove that both (particle and wave) are occurring at the same time.

It is the act of observation that makes it real! What if you were willing to observe yourself in more than one version of reality and then choose the one that pleases you most?

ASK FOR HELP

After you decide that you want to be in fifth dimension, then ask for help. At least once a day, I ask that my awareness be "in my fifth-dimensional self," and so can you. Ask for help from your angels, guides, and Ascended Masters. You can also ask the Hathors, fifth-dimensional beings of love and light from Venus. They carry the energy of unconditional love, so if you ask them to overshadow you and open your heart, they will help you. You will start acting from this lovely 5D way of being. If you need extra help, do the short and simple Hathor chant, *El Ka Leem Om,* which is the names of the four elements—earth, fire,

Figure 4.1. Hathor—this is the cover to the guided meditation CD,
Mantras for Ascension

water, and air—in the Hathor language, repeated over and over.* It is a very powerful tool for change.

EVOKE THE POWER OF DECISIONS TO HELP YOU STAY IN 5D

Almost everyone is in the situation of doing a balancing act between the third, fourth, and fifth dimensions. It's possible to be in 5D and then vacillate out. It's possible for your emotional body to become 5D, while your physical body hangs back in 3D. Sometimes it boils down to a single decision, such as activating one of the following possibilities, to be "part of the solution." Such decisions will greatly enhance your ability to stay in 5D more and more.

Bring Your God Energy into Everything

When I was growing up, we always blessed our food. Although this practice seems long forgotten in some households, it does change the items on your plate and infuses your consciousness, your ability to anchor divine energy or God energy into your food! In fact, my father, a devout Catholic and greenhouse grower, asked the priest to come and bless the crops with every planting. Blessing can be done with every action—reading e-mails, grocery shopping, doing your daily tasks! Decide to bless the action, asking for its highest vibrational expression. Do this with a simple prayer, such as, "Dear God, please bless me while I open e-mails!"

Connect with the Elemental Kingdom

One of the easiest ways to find your way into a fifth-dimensional expression is to take a walk in nature. Look for reasons to find beauty. Maybe it's the sunrise or sunset; maybe it's a beautiful flower or tree. Whatever

---

*You will find supplemental instructions on this amazing chant on track 2 of the CD, *Mantras for Ascension,* listed in the Suggested Resources section of this book.

it is, give yourself to the moment of admiration; that will enable you to have a transcendent experience of appreciation and beauty. As you shift to recognize the importance of nature, your heart opens.

Magnify this everywhere you go. When you see something beautiful in nature, comment on it out loud to yourself or your companions. "I love that tree." "It's so beautiful." As you move into appreciation, you begin to see that you are part of something much bigger than yourself, and can easily move into fifth dimension. What follows is a discovery that nature can communicate with you.

Nature spirits hear you. As you become more fifth dimensional, you will perceive that nature elements are communicating with you—and are listening to you! During the great Golden Ages humans communicated with every living thing on the planet. You will develop a rapport with nature that allows you to make requests in the future. This is important. Nature spirits thrive on feedback from humans. If you have an outdoor garden area, consider creating an appreciation corner. To do this, place a little cup of treats for the elemental kingdom (gnomes, fairies, and elves) outside, hidden under a bush or plant. It should contain whole raw nuts, quality wrapped chocolate, or dried fruit such as figs, dates, or apricots. They will find it and get the message you are sending: "I am grateful for your service to me."

Invite them to help you and always ask for their help and appreciate them out loud whenever you notice the beauty of nature around you. I learned this the hard way when I was mentally complaining about the condition of my garden, reminding the elementals they were supposed to help me. That day they corrected me by saying, "You never asked us!" After I swallowed hard on humble pie, I asked, "If I ask you, will you help me?" They replied, "If we help you, will you still come into the garden all the time?" From that point forward I made a decision to take all my meals outside. In Wisconsin, that meant from March through the end of October. A little chill never stopped me! In the places I live now, it is still a priority!

The Hathor Chant will increase your receptivity in this area. There are many courses and books on the subject of communication with the nonspeaking elements of nature. If this stretches your belief about what is possible, then I encourage you to look into it further for yourself.

Work with Your Dreams

Dreamtime training will assist with your transformation. Many individuals do not remember their dreams. Some do not remember because they are going so far out into consciousness that there truly is no dream. However, if you do have dreams, keep a dream journal and write them out. Write questions after them, so you can see if you spontaneously get more information. For example, "I dreamt of a butterfly and then realized I have butterfly wings. Does that mean I've transformed?"

Meditate

Meditation is another way to rejuvenate the body. Becoming 5D necessitates that you find time, energy, and focus to meditate! If you cannot do your own meditations, take tips from the numerous guided mediations of many experts to help you discover the experience and bliss that comes from this practice. There is more information on meditation throughout the book and in great detail in chapter 10, "Becoming Fifth Dimensional and Activating the Higher Chakras."

One meditation anyone can do is the Facing the Sun meditation, which will provide you with a tremendous amount of the "breath of life." It will help you reach your ideal weight and give you a tremendous energy adjustment.

❋ FACING THE SUN OR SUN EATING MEDITATION

Many native cultures have used sun gazing to increase vitality and spirituality. You can damage your eyes staring at the sun so you must go very slowly. Ideally you will find a teacher who can guide you through the process.

Initially you will only look at the sun for five to ten seconds. Ideally you will have your feet flat on the ground without shoes. Gaze at the sun just as it rises or just before it sets. Think loving thoughts about yourself, life, the planet, and the sun. Better still, hold gratitude in your heart.

Each day you may increase your gazing by five to ten seconds. If your eyes hurt or the sun burns, go backward on your schedule a few days and work the length of time up again. If you do this daily, increasing your sun gazing no more than ten seconds each day, it will take you approximately nine months to achieve forty-four minutes. Once you reach forty-four minutes you are done. Do not rush or act needy or stressed in any way. Slow and steady is appropriate. Relax, allow, and center yourself. Enjoy the moment of thinking of nothing but pure love.

You do not need to do both, morning and evening. In fact it is preferable if you only gaze once a day. Some teachers believe that the sunrise is more potent than sunset. But if sunsets are what is possible for you, then that's your choice. Pick the one that works for you. Even if you cannot create a month-long program of sun eating, you can use this knowledge when you are able to view the sunset. Never stare directly at the sun at any other time of day. You could damage your eyes.

You can also use the free, guided meditations that come with this book. Website links can be found in the Suggested Resources section at the back. These meditations will invite the cosmic energies that are now available to move you into a new space. They will help you activate your DNA changes and speed up your evolution. These cosmic energies are changing who you are and allowing you to shift to higher frequencies.

Be Playful

As we shift into 5D, we must remember that we are not doing things "better." Were that true, it would mean that our former behavior wasn't good enough! This is a time to find and use nonpolarizing, nonpejorative words to describe new and different choices and experiences. The most profound shift will occur in the way you operate—the way you think—and you will discover that you do not need to "work." Rather, you need to be playful. Take a break when you get too overloaded with ideas. If you are not having fun, then you cannot stay in 5D, as it is a joyful place! Allow yourself to release attachments, expectations, and judgments so you can stay in 5D.

REJUVENATION OF THE BODY, MIND, AND SOUL

There are many ways of tapping into the rays of rejuvenation that are coming in to assist humanity. One way is simply to claim this! Repeat to yourself:

Rays of rejuvenation, rays of love, rays of 5D energy are rolling in, through, and around me! Saturate me and saturate the Earth with these rays—so that all of life may benefit.

Expand the Use of Healing Modalities

For example, over twenty years ago, while on a bike ride with a group of people, including my son, I rode my bike over an angled railroad crossing, and it caught in the railing. I went head over heels three times before stopping. My ten-year-old son came up to me where I lay in a crumpled heap, asking if I was all right.

Then he asked if I had any *Arnica montana* (a common homeopathic remedy for bruises and falls). Even though I normally carry it with me everywhere, I didn't have it. "That's too bad," he said, as I pulled myself together, getting back on my bike. Mentally I heard, "Imagine taking it." I did that, pretending to take a dose of the little pellets. I came away from that fall without a single bruise!

Unhook from Aging

Right now we are facing a "programming" of mass consciousness, which causes aging to occur. You can reverse the causes and ideas for aging by unhooking from mass consciousness beliefs about aging. Do yourself a favor and do everything you can to reclaim your divine mastery in all areas. You can empower your cells to pull their programming from another healthy version of you! In fact, you can work with your divine blueprint and set your ideal age. Keep the wisdom, and unhook from aging!

You can activate your full spectrum of DNA. Jean Adrienne is an author who has brought forth physical images to activate your 142 DNA strands. Using her card deck—*Reconnecting Soul: 142 DNA Activation Cards*—will effortlessly elevate you and your consciousness. You might not notice anything different, unless you keep a journal or other point of reference.

Also, stop referring to when things occurred and instead just refer to them when you need to! When you use dates, you are anchoring yourself into the mass consciousness programming about aging. When someone says she is getting old, or older, you can opt out easily by saying, "Speak for yourself!"

All resentment is a form of resistance to that which will keep you young. When you preserve your right (entitlement) to withhold love, your ego is establishing its territory by validating the past. This is what ages you and retards your progress to becoming fifth dimensional.

So how do you maintain your youthfulness? You begin by creating a desire, pure and simple. You use your intention that this is what you really want. Then begin to understand that it is already in you and you are simply falling in line with another version of you, a much younger, less-disappointed-in-life you. This may include accessing your new Crystal DNA. (One tool for this is the Crystal Elohim CD.) Next you adopt a pattern, a decision, to always be in integrity. Maintaining alignment in your thought, word, and action is a form of constancy that allows you to create anything you desire. Then see your desire in your mind's eye. Practice, practice, practice.

Go Beyond Mind-Altering Substances

Drugs by themselves will make you aware of higher dimensions, but without the attunement of the body, mind, and spirit, and without releasing your habitual response patterns. This means that if you don't meditate and just use drugs to alter your mind state, you will know about other worlds, but you won't truly be able to use the knowledge or understanding of higher states of consciousness. Meditation is necessary to bring about the alignment of your four lower bodies—physical, mental, emotional, and etheric—in such a way as to allow the pathways of information and experience to be open. The four lower bodies exist around your body in layers. When the bodies are lined up, connected, and communicating with each other you are in alignment.

Each of the four lower bodies has a specific purpose. You can touch and feel your physical body, the etheric body resides energetically just outside of the physical body as an energy shaped like your body. When a person has an out-of-body experience and still observes his or her body he or she is moving around in the etheric body. Your etheric body is home to your chakras and is your link to your Higher Self. Next, going outward, is the emotional body, the receptor of all your emotions, past and present. Emotions are energy that holds a purpose or feeling. Emotions must be expressed to be cleared of the purpose. The mental body holds the energy of the mind and all thought processes. This is also the source of creative power and manifestation.

Meditation to align these bodies makes the enlightenment of consciousness a permanent state of being, not simply a transitory experience, as with drugs. Meditation is an ongoing process and not something that one does just once or occasionally.

Synchronicity

Synchronicity is a valuable tool to help you understand reality. A term invented by Carl Jung, it refers to when two unrelated causes seem to produce simultaneity and meaning. It is dependent upon you, the observer, to see this. For example, if you see a billboard, or a license plate, or a printed sign that gives you the answer to something you have been contemplating, that is a synchronicity. When you hear a song in your head that doesn't seem to go away, and matches the feelings you are having or an event that happens shortly after the song appears, that's a synchronicity.

For example, a woman I know kept hearing lyrics from the song "Hands" by Jewel. "In the end, only kindness matters" went through her mind all morning. She was fired right after lunch! She chose to stay calm, sweet, and kind—even while being fired.

Synchronicity is more and more prevalent. Why? I believe it is because the universe wants us to know what we need to know, and our paying attention to it produces that result! We get to know!

CLAIM "NO MORE KARMA!"

Gone are the days where you need another chance to learn how to do something. You can now claim, with certainty, no more karma. In fact, the sooner you do it the better, because those who would hold you back are hoping you don't figure this one out! In fact, if this is the first time you are hearing this message, consider deciding that this is so for you. Everything will shift for you in an instant. Claim it: "Karma is over for me." It is part of the new paradigm of becoming fifth dimensional. This means that if you are angry with someone for stealing from you, or hurting you, you need to decide it doesn't matter. Don't decide to forgive, because forgiving means you are still holding them in a place of judgment. This new paradigm means that you can no longer hold energy against another—because then it is *you* that is holding the karma in place—not them. Yikes!

Because karma has ended, once you claim this you will be able to see beyond the veil. If you cling to your judgment of another, you won't see beyond the veil of illusion. This will cause you to become locked into a system of believing there is nothing more than physical experience. This feeds those who would hold you back. Once you have claimed the end of karma, then you are "off the matrix" of delusion. No one can fool you or trick you any more.

One of the ways to ensure your success in this area is to practice the

Crystal Elohim Meditation.* I highly recommend you use this empowering energetic tool. It will greatly expand your abilities, your consciousness, and your fifth-dimensional expression. The Elohim are cosmic energies that will support your Ascension work. They channeled this guided meditation for the CD. The Elohim channeled this meditation to me in 1994. They insisted at that time that I drop everything and create the guided meditation. The Crystal Elohim Meditation will take you to many realms, both past and present, and even to the beginnings of creation. It will enable you to connect with the source codes of creation and create new matrices for yourself.

One meditator said, "I immediately began to feel my body vibrate to a higher frequency at the molecular level. As a result, I became lighter and experienced an incredible expansiveness." This meditation will anchor into your field (four lower bodies) the crystalline grids from higher dimensions. Humanity is changing from carbon-based DNA to crystalline DNA. There are grids around the planet for every living thing. In addition, there are dissolving grids that expressed the old polarity matrix along with grids that programmed humanity to stay in its old dysfunctional way. There are many aspects of these grids that are not fully understood by anyone. The grids that are behind the original creation were of the purest form. Many have seen the Christ-conciousness grid whose purpose is to assist humankind in becoming the perfected human, or Christed one.

The Crystal Grids

The crystal grids are replacing all the old dysfunctional grids of the planet. Over the past five years many new grids have been created by the Ascended Masters, the extraterrestrials of the light, and certain light workers such as me for the purpose of reestablishing humanity's birthright. Many of you are now between grids of the third and fourth dimen-

---

*For more on the Crystal Elohim Meditation see Suggested Resources. The meditation itself has little gaps for the listener to repeat and participate. It is extremely powerful to amp up your DNA and connects you to crystal DNA.

sions and are not really plugged into the magnetics of the fifth and higher dimensions. This is why you can be tired and spacy as you shift between grids that held you back and those that help you move forward.

These new grids have replaced old, perverted patterns that were in place to hold humanity back. Each illness, human mental dysfunction, and the like had grids that projected on to humans. The new grids are part of the original templates and are the authentic codes and patterns for our fifth-dimensional expression. They will enable you to detach from the mass consciousness 3D grids that have you locked into behaviors that no longer serve you. Just like you might use many resources to find a doctor, or a carpenter, using the crystal grid allows you to gain mastery and wisdom beyond your current knowing.

To learn and use the grids, you may make a request to find solutions to specific problems. Initially, think of how any master plan helps to produce, contain process and progress, and define outcomes. This grid or master plan for what you may be attempting to produce in yourself already exists in higher dimensions and will be activated for you. It's like connecting your cell phone to a cell phone tower. You know you have a connection because your calls go through. Knowing that the answer already exists in a creation pattern and asking to connect to such a grid will suffice.

Ideally, you'll use these grids to activate your higher knowing, to inspire your creativity, to enliven your relationships, and to evolve who you are. Tune to these grids. Be willing to contribute your experiences and to expand your consciousness. Connecting to these grids is a simple matter in your meditations.

First get into a meditation position, in a location that allows you to be peaceful and quiet for at least thirty minutes. You may sit, stand, or lie down.

Allow yourself to expand your awareness to fill the space around your heart. Then increase this awareness to the field of energy around your body.

Let yourself acknowledge your energy bodies and expand this awareness as you explore each of your energy bodies. Move your attention to the edges of your own physical body.

Then imagine the next body, the etheric body. It expands beyond your physical body by a few inches. Imagine this is a beautiful, electric blue cloudlike shape following the shape of your physical body.

Next, imagine the emotional body as a beautiful pink field around the body even larger still.

Finally, imagine your mental body surrounding these bodies. It has an iridescent quality. It can be any color, although it is primarily whitish.

You are now ready to expand your own energy to the size of the grid around the Earth. Imagine your specific agenda or issue has a grid already in existence, ready to solve your issue or idea. (This is possible because a higher version of you knows what you are looking for and creates it before you can request it.) Intend that it find you and connect with you.

See your etheric body connecting to this grid, receiving information and updating your own four lower bodies. You may also be a contributor to these grids in much the same way, by intending your mastery be exchanged or transferred while you are also receiving any new information that you may require.

It is very important that you hold the purest of intention when you are purposefully working with the grids. Be aware that your dark thoughts and emotional imbalances could misalign you or a segment of the grid. Ask the angels to purify your actions when working with the grid so that you are always in alignment with God. Purity of heart is the most important element of the grid.

These crystal templates and the Crystal Elohim will create a much higher level of expression for you.* When the tide goes up, all the ships in the harbor rise. Similarly, these new grids make it easier for you to be your most evolved self. You will assist yourself and humanity by access-

---

*The Crystal Elohim sprang forth from the seven mighty Elohim as mankind was beginning to move into the great golden age.

ing this information and expressing it. Your vibration will then amplify the information on the grids so it is easier for others around you to adopt these higher vibrations, these higher expressions. This is how humanity will assist each other in becoming fifth dimensional.

It is important to note that this process is occurring planetary-wide. Not only is humanity evolving, but so is the Earth. Furthermore, these two evolutions are codependent. This means that your efforts are exponentially increased because they influence all of humanity and the cosmos.

Sacred Geometry and Metatron's Star

Understanding sacred geometry will greatly aid your abilities to shift and adjust to the fifth-dimensional you. Sacred geometry, the study of mathematical ratios, harmonics, and proportion, can be found throughout the cosmos in music, light, and design. Discovering divine expressions of sacred proportion throughout nature unlocks and activates codes in you that allow you to access your divine wisdom.

Robert Lawler coined the term *sacred geometry*. He wrote the "bible" of sacred geometry, wherein he identifies the ratios and geometry found throughout nature, the human body, and celestial bodies. The most significant of these ratios is the golden mean or *phi*. This relationship is found in the DNA spiral, bones, plants, and celestial bodies. Artists for centuries have used these relationships to create pleasing structures and art. It is a known, researched fact that humans prefer the golden mean to any other proportion.

Sacred geometry is one of the incredibly powerful tools that help humanity to unlock the codes of the universe. It has become the subject of hundreds of books because it represents so many different kinds of information from nature to art to physics. Accessing this information will aid your progress in becoming fifth dimensional. Looking at mandala art, learning about sacred geometry, or using it in meditation are just a few of the powerful uses of this magical study. It is an essential aspect of the MerKaBa Classic meditation.

One particular example of mandala art can be seen in the flower of life symbol or Metatron's star.* Metatron's star, or Metatron's cube, as it is more commonly known, is the circle of circles based on the same size circle being placed around a center circle. This is easy to imagine, if you start with thirteen coins of the same size. Put one in the middle, then surround it with six coins, then extend those six coins one more coin so you create a six-pointed star. This shape produces all the Platonic solids: the tetrahedron, cube, octahedron, icosahedron, and dodecahedron. The Platonic solids are considered sacred geometry because humans have awakened to the scientific understanding that all geometry, all chemistry, and all of nature are based on these five sacred forms. Each of the sacred forms can be created from connecting the centers of the thirteen spheres in the formation of Metatron's star.

Although Metatron's star is not the same as the "flower of life" symbol (in fig. 4.2), it is the source code for that symbol. Metatron's star

Figure 4.2.
Flower of life

---

*Metatron described himself in this way to me in a channeling: "I am a cosmic being, sitting at the right hand of God. I oversee the archangels who are evolving as well as the entire angelic realm. My mission is to maintain the integrity of all material form. Metatron's cube was named after me, because it contains the exact source code of all things manifest. It is the perfected source of light."

contains the additional completed circles that are often missing in the symbol of the flower of life. Those missing circles are implied, so the flower of life symbol implies the full matrix. It contains the seed of all life moving through the cosmos. Looking at the symbol, wearing it, or visualizing it affirms your agreement with all of life that this is source code; this is your divine template.

The bees are connected with this divine blueprint by virtue of the matrix where they build their hive. They carry this imprint to everything they touch, including the pollen, which allows the divine blueprint to be reignited in every living thing that bees pollinate. Whenever you see a bee at work, offer your blessings and your gratitude and also call upon Metatron and Archangel Michael* to protect these elementals (the bees) that are so very important to all of life on this planet.

You can use the flower of life symbol, or Metatron's star/cube for healing. You might wear flower of life jewelry. You can place the symbol over the affected area of the body. You can put it under your plants or under your dinner plate. If your entire body needs healing, put the flower of life symbol over a photograph of your entire body. Practice drawing it. Then color it. Do this over and over. Start with a good compass, or better yet, use an old compact disc that you can trace and mark the center of easily.

CONFIRMATION OF YOUR CONNECTION

As you become more and more tuned to your body, you will notice sensations that confirm your consistent connection with the fifth dimension. You will also experience aches and pains as your body seeks to eliminate anything that could hold you back. If you have consulted a

---

*As the overseer of the archangels, Metatron works closely with Archangel Michael. Michael is the protector and defender of life and the will of God on planet Earth. He is identified in seven of the world's religions, including the three major religions of Christianity, Islam, and Judaism. In the Islamic tradition, he is considered the angel of nature providing food and knowledge.

medical professional and he or she has found no medical cause, it is most likely that these are symptoms of your Ascension.

Body Confirmations

Your first communication from the Higher Self might be in what I call "body confirmations," which enable your body to tell you that you are in resonance with the divine version of you.

The traditional one that almost everyone gets is goose bumps or goose flesh (also known as goose pimples or chill bumps): the little bumps that show up on your skin, usually on your arms and legs, right at the hair follicle; they last just a few seconds. When you get body confirmation, it is a powerful yet simple "sign" that your body is in resonance with your words (or someone else's words in the moment).

It is an exciting experience when you say what you are thinking or "getting" in the moment, and you or someone near you gets goose bumps! It's the universe telling you to keep up the good work, that you are on to something! Pay attention to what you just said when this happens. Debbie Ford, American self-help author well known for *The Dark Side of the Light Chasers,* called them "God Bumps."

Everyone experiences these symptoms differently. One of my students in a class felt an itch on her ear when the Higher Self came through, but she didn't like it so she dismissed it. Then her foot itched. "That couldn't be it either" was her thought, so then her whole body itched! She decided to take the itchy ear as her "yes" symbol! What's even more revealing is that she was black and a white woman sitting across from her in class had the identical experience. They compared notes and were able to determine that they were from the same energetic family group and vowed to stay in touch! What great synergy, having a soul sister show up this way.

Some Other Symptoms

Here's a short list of other symptoms you may experience, and some suggestions for coping with them.

Night sweats—There is not much you can do about this, other than determine nothing else is wrong, and try to be as comfortable as possible.

Waking up after just three hours of sleep—Be productive, meditate, read, and write. Then go back to sleep after being awake for thirty to fifty minutes.

Strange food cravings—Follow them; they may surprise you. On the other hand, you may develop antipathy to certain foods (which might have additives or products that aren't at your vibration)!

Irritability—Usually this comes from an entity that has taken up residence. Do clearing work, a process where you cast out unwanted energies or disembodied spirits that do not belong in your body.

Repeated patterns keep surfacing—This means it's time to do something about it! Seek learning tools that will help you eliminate the "holdbacks" coming from past life issues along with emotional blockages and external energies.*

Feeling spacy, or out of it—First make sure nothing is wrong with you, seeing a doctor or visiting the emergency room if you do not feel well. You may need grounding work (as described earlier in this book; see page 9). Or you may be working at higher levels and just need to take a break, have a nap, or relax.

---

*In her groundbreaking *Remarkable Healings,* psychotherapist Dr. Shakuntala Modi discovered unsuspected roots of mental and physical illness and a method to cast out these energies. The book contains detailed stories of these remarkable healings. Another well-developed method of healing emotions and family issues along with ancestry is known as Family Constellation work, founded by German therapist Bert Hellinger. It is based on the concept that guilt and lack of acceptance drive the individual to seek to belong. Also the Emotion Code and Body Code energy healing was developed by Dr. Bradley Nelson to address a myriad of physical issues with their underlying causes that may include past lives and trapped emotions. There are many trained professionals in each of these modalities. I am familiar with and exposed to their tremendous healing capabilities and recommend these therapies in general.

Physical pain—This is something that you must pay attention to. Go to a doctor and get checked out. Or go to the emergency room! Pay attention to the physical part of your life and determine causes where possible.

If your inner guidance says, "Nothing is wrong," that's OK. However, if you are unsure, then you must get it checked out. My clients have had physical pain of all sorts occur that is unrelated to any physical ailment. It had everything to do with "upgrades," meaning that you are adjusting to higher frequencies that are moving through your body as you become more fifth dimensional. This is another reason you must do your part and learn your Higher Self connection, so that you can verify the information that you are getting!

In the Akashic Records work, I began to notice that certain signs would show up to confirm a person's connection to the Akashic Records. Some Akashic guides, individuals who have trained to open the Akashic Records of a client, experience a pressure on the chest (heart chakra), or a pulsing (very subtle), or a soundless sound (like white noise, and not tinnitus). When you have been trained to recognize them, these tools serve as markers that you have anchored into the energy known as the Akashic Records. These feelings verify that your connection is secure and clear! In addition, I sometimes feel something that is going on with a client in my physical body. I do not consider myself a medical intuitive, but in the Akashic Records I often have received physical sensations that mirrored the client's own issues.

A Visual Sign of 5D

One time, while reading for a client in another country and working with a translator, I asked for a few moments to connect with her before we brought the client into the conference. I asked my Akashic Records guides to be replicated over my translator, so she would "know" instantly the correct translation of the material that was coming forward. What happened next was amazing! I saw a beautiful purple beam of light overshadow my translator (while we were on Skype!). I couldn't figure out how to take a picture on Skype so I grabbed my phone and took her picture.*

---

*The photo is available in the resources section of my website, so you can see the purple energy beam in full color.

Orbs

There have been several books and discussions on orbs, and many of you have had orbs in your photos and wondered why they are appearing now. Orbs are those little white or colored spheres that sometimes show up in photos. In truth they have always been there, but now your vibration is expanding to include higher dimensional awareness. This is why our cameras are showing us visuals that most do not see with the naked eye. These energies have always been there and are now being photographed by people who are fourth dimensional or higher. When the fifth-dimensional person is in the photo or is the photographer, the orbs show up. This is another sign that we are expanding our awareness, our consciousness, to vibrate at the level of the higher dimensions.

Handling Uncomfortable Symptoms

As you shift to higher dimensions, you may experience certain health issues that are related to physical changes in the body. These changes may take the form of sudden leaps in symptoms. If this is happening to you, keep in mind that *rest* is the most important element.

You may have old emotional wounds or be healing past lifetimes, or you might even be healing for the planet. For sure, you are not alone. Many who are going through these changes experience high blood pressure, joint aches and pains, headaches, and more. Many a light worker, like you, or anyone who is interested in saving the Earth or the people thereon, accepts "double duty," picking up related traumas to help clear the Earth. If you are feeling uncomfortable, especially if you are in pain, you might be tempted to try to "beg off" the Ascension process. You might have said, "This is just too much for me. I cannot do it, or I don't want to be here!" This is why asking for help is so valuable. If you don't want to ask for help, it may create a much slower process.

You must follow your inner guidance in this area as well as get help from practitioners that can serve you. There are many new types of therapy that are appropriate. You can consider individuals who will help you heal past traumas to the physical body, which carry over from other lifetimes. If you are suffering and do not know what is going on—and the medical profession has not been able to assist you—then check out the list of suggested healing modalities found earlier in this chapter (page 80).

If you are in physical pain, recite the mantra, "Does it have to hurt?" over and over until the pain abates. It may be incomprehensible to you that your angels and guides do not know how much pain you are in—but they don't! They are not in a body. They experience the bliss of God connection so continually that for them to feel your pain would be excruciating. Your mantra, "Does it have to hurt?" actually assists them in calibrating with you so your symptoms can be lessened to the degree of tolerance.

IT MAY BE INCOMPREHENSIBLE TO YOU THAT YOUR ANGELS AND GUIDES DO NOT KNOW HOW MUCH PAIN YOU ARE IN— BUT THEY DON'T! THEY ARE NOT IN A BODY. THEY EXPERIENCE THE BLISS OF GOD CONNECTION SO CONTINUALLY THAT FOR THEM TO FEEL YOUR PAIN WOULD BE EXCRUCIATING.

You might be called to be a healer, or you might first learn certain tools to heal yourself and then find that your work as a healer or intuitive has been activated, so that you develop your personal version of this healing work for clients. If you are already in these arenas, you might be accelerated. Some have even reported knowing information about others that they did not ask for!

MAKING GOD CHOICES

When you are 5D there is no free will. What could this mean? In 3D you have the God choice, or the not-God choice. The not-God choice is the equivalent of making mistakes or sins. Think of a little child you are the guardian for who goes outside with you after a big rainstorm. What will that child do? Find a puddle and jump in it! You're going to let him play—and then when it is all over, you give him a bath, and wash his clothes. Everything is fine. That's like us in 3D—we get dirty, and then we go back to God and become clean again.

The free will zone isn't needed anymore because at 5D you only want a God choice. A point of maturity exists at 5D because the God choice is so attractive that you don't need the Ten Commandments; it wouldn't occur to you to steal or lie or covet. Your God love would be so pervasive that it would please you immensely to make a God choice. When you are faced with a decision that society might say is ethically challenging, you intuitively dismiss any not-God choice. Take the example of meeting someone you really are attracted to and then discovering that he or she is married; the idea of being involved just won't come up. (This is, of course, presuming you are not available as a romantic partner to anyone who is married, which is a conscious choice.) Because you are not available to married persons, you are not tempted to cross the line. You are able to communicate this with absolute sincerity, kindness, and patience. It comes out of you in a very gentle way and is a very powerful experience.

In 5D it's more like this—think of a person you admire, maybe the Dalai Lama. Imagine that I phone you and tell you he needs a place to stay and he doesn't want a hotel. I've checked my database and your location is perfect. What will you say? Yes, of course! This is because you wouldn't think of passing up a chance to be in the presence of someone that special. It's a fabulous opportunity. I might ask if there's anything else you need to know. Your questions might be around what kind of food he likes, if he will be traveling alone, and the dates he is coming. All those questions are on the side of "yes." The possibility of saying "no" doesn't occur to you. You are so connected to God that you only desire a God choice; only an expression of love is possible.

Everyone is becoming fifth dimensional. Enough people have brought the transition in that there is no going back. We also have the full support of the Ascended Masters, the entire angelic realm, the Great White Brotherhood,* and God. Yes, God's presence has moved directly into this region of reality. It is an awesome presence. It will make it so much easier to be who you really are. God's love and nurturing will help you feel safe and able to be your best self.

---

*H. P. Blavatsky and Nicholas and Helena Roerich in their works *Isis Unveiled* and *Hierarchy* (respectively) describe the Great White Brotherhood as a group of immortals who maintain an active watch over the world from their risen place as Ascended Masters. The group is also known as Great Brotherhood of Light or the Spiritual Hierarchy of Earth.

5
Your Emotions
Carry the Key

Your emotions are what make you uniquely human. On this planet, emotions are a significant part of the experience of life. Emotions are *chi* (energy) that has been imbued with a purpose. Although mental prowess may make you feel superior, in truth your use of emotions can help you achieve more than your mind can. Your emotions are the key to the world around you; they "read" the field for you—faster and more accurately than the mind. Your emotional body reads the emotional bodies of those around you and signals when you are unsafe or loved, cherished or feared, and so on. Think of the phrases, "I had a sinking feeling in my gut" or "My heart leapt for joy." These phrases are keys that can hold you back or move you forward. You see how very accurate your emotions are and how useful they can be to understand the reality around you.

Contrary to popular thinking, the dimensions are nested inside each other.* From any point within the dimensions you can see into the lower ones. At each acquired level of discernment, you then have the capacity to observe the lower vibratory ones. This is also why you don't necessarily notice when you are in fourth dimension because third

---

*I carry this information from the Akashic Records, from my guides, and from my Higher Self.

dimension is so close and so real; you are concurrently experiencing both. The lower dimensions are not lesser, like fewer dollars, but lower, as in vibration, as pitch can be higher or lower in music. Which pitch is better? Hopefully the answer is obvious: *none.* They are all important. Each serves a purpose.

Thus, as you become more fifth dimensional, you are able to see and understand the polarity in both fourth and third dimensions without experiencing an emotional charge. You observe, without judgment. As you gain mastery of experiencing emotion, and then stepping back away from it as the observer, you can notice your emotions. As the observer, you can choose to approach polarity experiences with compassion, which will allow you to instantly become fifth dimensional. As you integrate third- and fifth-dimensional expressions, you will have a uniquely powerful mastery of your emotions.

This means when someone does something to hurt you, first you feel the pain. Then you notice her actions and your feelings about her actions. You may or may not have reactions. All this is done without judging. You may even experience a "blow to the heart," when someone close to you does something shocking and hurtful, and it causes you to feel pain because you have expectations that aren't being met. These expectations may be honest, real, fair, or not. Expectations between close associates are a normal part of these relationships. Learn to understand your own expectations, so that when someone does let you down, you can move quickly through your disappointment and pain, understanding your part of the drama. A blow to the heart is rocket fuel to your Ascension work. It is one key to becoming fifth dimensional.

As you incorporate your fifth-dimensional self into who you are, your emotions are just as important as they were before. In fact, they are more so! The difference is that you don't have the need to rework them, or overwork them. Instead, you can look upon the emotions as a vehicle for expanding your awareness of expression, experience, and feelings. Your emotions give you a full connection to your heart (if you allow it). Your emotions can magnify your state of high or low. This gives you the greatest possible opportunity to unify your fifth-dimensional self with your third-dimensional self.

MISUSE AND CONTROL OF EMOTIONS

Your emotions can only react once, but your mind can rerun that emotion, causing you to suffer by replaying a scenario, reinvigorating the emotions, and causing any pain and suffering to be felt over and over. It's like picking at a wound that is trying to heal. Why not use your happy emotions to make magic? What if you couldn't replay some difficult experience? What if your memory could only produce data, and not replays of emotions?

It is a known fact among "those who would hold you back" that humanity's emotions are powerful tools to create reality. All of the feelings of anger, rage, disappointment, and fear can be used to manipulate you. When you maintain your state of compassion, you cannot be manipulated; you cannot be used for fuel in ways that you may not yet understand.

. . . .

YOUR EMOTIONS CAN ONLY REACT ONCE, BUT YOUR MIND
CAN RERUN THAT EMOTION, CAUSING YOU TO SUFFER BY
REPLAYING A SCENARIO, REINVIGORATING THE EMOTIONS,
AND CAUSING ANY PAIN AND SUFFERING TO BE FELT
OVER AND OVER. WHAT IF YOU COULDN'T REPLAY SOME
DIFFICULT EXPERIENCE? WHAT IF YOUR MEMORY COULD
ONLY PRODUCE DATA, AND NOT REPLAYS OF EMOTIONS?
WOULD YOU SUFFER LESS?

. . . .

On the other hand, the desire to use the mind to control the emotions doesn't serve you anymore. Instead, allow your emotions a voice. Give up suppressing them. Validate the self. Let go of the need to be vindicated by others. Instead, honor your suffering and move on. Then move your pain through your heart, flooding it with unconditional love for yourself and others. Your job is not to eliminate the mind but to integrate the emotions and the intellect and move all of it through your heart. This truly is the threefold flame of love, wisdom, and power. This is symbolized by the fleur-de-lis, often seen as a symbol for France and the symbol of the Merovingians, the family descended from Mary Magdalene.

Know this: your state of joy is your best ammunition with which to respond to anything that occurs to you that you do not like. In the 3D state, "Don't get mad, get even" might be the response. Now that we are waking up in 5D we can say, "Don't get mad, be happy." Sincere, true happiness is empowering. Don't take your inexperience for failure to be happy. Be happy in spite of any difficulty. You will attract more happiness. The veils are thinning, and you are becoming more powerful daily. Use this to your advantage.

EMOTIONS THAT HOLD YOU BACK

What kinds of emotions hold you back? See the list below.

Resentment—the energy of blame

Fear—the energy of incongruence

Whining—the energy of self-validation

Self-righteousness—the energy of bitterness and claiming, "This is how it is."

Denial—the energy of separateness (as contrasted to oneness)

The Role of Judgment

Many do not realize they carry judgment in almost every thought. Judgments about the goodness or badness of a situation, or behavior or outcome, infect your thoughts and cause you to freeze-frame these situations. Your mind immediately moves into, "Well, I would do it this way. . . ." Decide to notice when you start this internal dialog. Decide to encourage others to do what pleases them. When they ask you what to do, "What pleases you?" can be your response.

What if you could feel a judgment starting to form and then notice, "Oh, I'm having expectations here that aren't being met." Once you notice the evidence of expectation you can laugh at yourself and let go of the expectation and move out of judgment.

The Role of Guilt

Guilt has one good use, to guide you to choose differently next time. Those who would hold you back have harnessed it to keep you locked into believing you aren't good enough or smart enough. What does guilt do to you? It locks many into a belief system that proves someone else is right and their own behavior or choices are wrong. There is no need for guilt in 5D, because the minute you discover another way of doing things, you choose differently. The energy shifts and changes instantaneously without your judging your prior actions as good or bad! In fact, in this zone, you don't really mind what your choices were last time.

Guilt is another form of judgment. It is worse, because there's no other observer except you, and it becomes insidious in your thought. The whole purpose of guilt is to inspire you to be different. Unresolved guilt becomes self-judgment. Generally we don't like to live with self-judgment, so we project it outward to others.

When you carry guilt, these feelings can actually be based on old beliefs about how you are supposed to act or how others should behave. When you project them onto others, these emotions of self-judgment become the coatrack on which you hang everyone else's guilt. This is a false belief based around a wound, a wound that you could heal. Typically a wound is held in place by the perpetrator who has become the placeholder validating your pain. Why do you need to continue to validate your pain? Is it because you don't value yourself? Decide to notice your blame toward yourself or others and see where you are holding wounds! Sometimes it isn't until someone actually activates your wound that you notice you were holding energy in that area, and then you can do something about it.

The Role of Blame and Whining

Blame and whining are also a form of self-validation. They validate your pain and promote your victimhood. They seek acknowledgment to maintain the status quo, validating it, as it allows you to be stagnant rather than taking action on your misery.

You have a personal duty to validate yourself. Don't make someone else do that. It's okay to tell your story, but do so without blame. Various versions of "he done me wrong" give you validation for your experiences. It may get you sympathy for your wound and compensate you for your loss, but at what expense? It holds you where you are instead of helping you evolve! That's why you really only need to do it once.

Human nature usually leads us to tell our stories of being "wronged" over and over, playing into the victim mentality. This keeps us locked into third dimension, polarity consciousness. The "drama business" of TV reality shows is all about this! You are not doing yourself any favors by telling your story over and over. Instead, decide to tell your story up to three times. That's it. Keep track. With an internal retelling limit (of three), you might slip back into third dimension, but you won't stay there.

Why give "free rent" in your head to someone that you don't even want to spend time with? Anger or hatred gives energy to another, to behavior that you didn't like, and attracts more of the same!

Anger moved to blame is laziness. Blame keeps you lazy. Blame keeps you locked into the perpetual polarity of third dimension. It does this by holding you in victimhood. When you begin to see this and truly forgive, you forget. Then you have no reason to blame! Later, we will be discussing forgetfulness. Everyone is forgetting. It is quite amazing.

The Higher Self version of you (your fifth-dimensional self) doesn't judge the other party, as it doesn't need to. And in fifth dimension you don't remember past hurts, because in fifth dimension the self doesn't need validation. The self, when fully plugged into its God-centeredness, already *knows* itself to be loved unconditionally. You no longer need to remember past hurts because emotional wound memory isn't nearly as pleasing as the feeling of unconditional love that comes from your ever-present God connection. This moves you into the all-important now, your new normal.

When you heal the part of you that is critical and projects this criticism out to others, it is no longer a button to be pushed by you or others. Instead, you find their behavior entertaining or funny, as you are amused by their behaviors rather than annoyed. This is the way out of this Rubik's cube.

Why doesn't the fifth-dimensional energy need to judge? It does not need to be validated for loss or pain. Instead, it responds to loss with acceptance, knowing that loss and gain are two sides of an experience of limitation. The 5D self acknowledges that life is a dance of experiences and lets happiness reign. In 5D, validation for existence is constant; this is your God connection. This constant of being fully plugged into self awareness of the whole, the self-awareness of God, is so fulfilling that initially you will be content to experience just this. Soon enough you'll want to move into creation again. This may be mind boggling to you now, but once you've experienced this, you will be able to recognize it.

The Role of Bitterness

The role of bitterness is to keep you locked into evaluating the situation or circumstances that justify your anger, hatred, or pain. None of this serves you. None of it is real. In all cases you are either transmuting your own pain or the world's. Decide to let go of it and love anyway. It's a choice. Choosing wisely helps you anchor your fifth-dimensional energy. Bitterness is fostered by jealousy. You want what someone else has. An evolved moment came to me when I observed a good friend behaving badly and announced to someone else, "She thinks she's entitled." As soon as those words left my lips, I found myself saying, "I wonder what I am acting entitled to." I got the answer right away and acted on it immediately!

The Role of Fear

Fear will also show up in this transition zone, because its domain is fourth dimension. Fear is a messenger. Fear is a feeling that your emotional body creates to get you to change. Fear invites you to change your belief or change your behavior!

FEAR

- Fear is used to manipulate you.
- Fear keeps you locked in more fear.
- Fear is fuel for those who would have you fail.
- Fear is a messenger—chi loaded with a purpose—intended to keep you safe.
- Your emotional body creates fear.
- Fear warns you when something needs to change: either your behavior or your belief.
- Fear was created as an alarm system to tell you "something is not right." It's up to you to heed it.
- Ascended beings disguised as humans are those among us who are fearless and are meant to help you wake up to your divinity. If you are fearless, you're probably one of the Ascended Masters in embodiment.

Fear is a messenger that all systems in all dimensions are not aligned. When you are in alignment with yourself, in all of your expressions, you will be able to co-create as you were intended. It's not a problem when you are out of integrity; it just impedes your progression in the Ascension. If you are building a house, you don't throw rocks at the windows at night for entertainment. Choosing to be in integrity propels your progress.

One of the fastest ways to dissolve fear is to speak to it directly, asking the question, "I can feel the fear; what is the message?" Once you know this information you are able to change your belief or change your behavior.

IF YOU ARE BURDENED BY YOUR FEARS ALL THE TIME,
TAKE THE TIME TO GET TO KNOW THEM. YOU WILL BE
SURPRISED THAT THEY ARE GENERALLY "PURPOSEFUL" ENERGY,
TRYING TO HELP YOU ACHIEVE YOUR GOALS AND DESIRES.
WHEN FEAR SHOWS UP, ASK FOR ITS MESSAGE, AND
THEN CHANGE YOUR BELIEF OR YOUR BEHAVIOR.

This is an important step toward becoming fifth dimensional. When you open your mind, you become creative. When you open your heart, you become compassionate. When the heart and mind are synchronized, they open the portal to 5D. Being fearless is an expression of this alignment. It occurs when your beliefs, thoughts, and actions are in alignment, producing integrity. When you know (not believe, but know) that you are responsible for your reality, then you will be fearless too.

TALKING TO FEAR AS THE MESSENGER

Consider the use of a simple meditation to address your fears. Speak to your fears as if they were messengers.

1. Take a moment now and close your eyes. Think of something you've felt fearful about. Acknowledge the fear.
2. Then ask the fear: "What's your message?"
3. Be open to receive it, and the information will come flooding through. Flooding? Yes. Why? Finally the emotion of fear will have fulfilled its true purpose: to serve as a messenger about the lack of congruency or the lack of alignment between your mind, words, and actions.

As you acquire the ability to meditate on your fear and learn of its message, you can then choose to change your belief or change your behavior.

FEAR AND FEARLESSNESS

Part of the success of "those who would hold you back" is the fear factor that causes you to think they have power over you. They don't. They are the interlopers. Be sure to get used to letting them know, "You don't belong here." My recommendation is to say it out loud, any time things are happening that cause you to be even a little bit afraid. "You have no power here, you don't belong here. Leave. Now." Say it with firmness, with conviction; say it like you mean it! This is especially true when unseen forces are leaving you uneasy!

You have choice. You do not have to put up with a life you don't like; you don't have to put up with fear. You do have to decide that it's your life, which you are going to take charge of.

Invoking the Mommy Clause

A client of mine told me the story of an entity that had taken over her son and caused him to move into heavy drug use. He was being admitted to the hospital with an apparent psychotic break. A psychic friend had informed the mom earlier that day that her son "had a contract with the entity" that was inside of him. The energy coming off him was strong and defiant. She sent her husband home from the emergency room, waited until the nurses were gone, and looked her son in the eye, saying, "Every contract has an exit clause. You just met the mommy clause. Get out now." She made a loud noise. Later, the doctor—who didn't know what she had done—told her everything had shifted.

Some people are born fearless. They are always congruent. They always see the "us" in situations instead of "me." These fearless ones are born innately connected to all of life and know what to do in times of danger, yet do not need to show off. They love humanity so much and see themselves as part of the whole. This "part of the whole" expression is not based in belief, but in consciousness. As a result they sometimes have trouble understanding those that don't see the all-encompassing "we" version of the reality that reveals the true nature of consciousness and expression. For example, as children, they may be a real challenge for their parents and family since they don't understand why all the toys don't belong to all the children.

These fearless ones are the Ascended Masters in embodiment at this time. Those of you who are reading this, who are already fearless, take note. It means you have a much bigger responsibility to humanity and the planet, because you came here not to learn lessons, not to fulfill a personal objective, but to assist in the planetary transformation. How will you do this? For starters, just show up. Honor your feelings, and you'll know.

Fearless in Atlanta

Back in the 1990s, before everyone had their own cell phones, I arrived in Atlanta and called my host from an airport phone. She asked if I would consider taking the MARTA (Metropolitan Atlanta Rapid Transit Authority) to the station near her home, as she was tied up in a meeting and couldn't get to the airport easily. I agreed. She said, "Be sure to call me when you get on the train." I didn't own a cell phone at the time but figured I could call her from the platform. Years earlier, when I lived in NYC, the subway platforms always had pay phones.

Once on the MARTA platform, I chose to take the train to my destination, without making the requested call to alert her, because there were no phones there. Two women got on the car and a very tall, large man got on the car. The two women got off. Now it was just me and the man in the transit car. I thought nothing of it. The man got up from his seat. Coming over to stand in front of me, he demanded that I give him some money.

"No, I'm not going to do that," I replied.

He persisted, "Just give me some money!"

"No," I said. Then I remembered I should have called my host and reasoned that I would pay him if I could borrow his cell phone if he had one. "Do you have a cell phone?" I asked.

"No!" came his angry response.

"Well, then, I'm not going to give you any money!"

"Just give me some money!" he demanded." "No."

I pointed to my suitcases and then my ears. "I mean no disrespect, I just got off a plane, and I'm having trouble hearing you. Are you asking me anything different than you just asked me a couple of minutes ago?" I said, my exasperation rising slightly.

"Just give me some money!"

By this time we pulled into the next station, and he headed toward the door, and I looked at him and said, "You might try sales; you are pretty persistent!" I wasn't afraid of him—in fact, I really didn't mind him one way or the other. This is fifth dimension. I had no fear of him because, although he was a bully, my emotional body could read that he wasn't going to harm me. I didn't think about it. I didn't need to. It was only from a third-dimensional perspective that I could see the implications of the event. I didn't make any excuses to him; I didn't say, "I don't have any." At fifth dimension you have no need for lies—even little ones.

RECOGNIZING AND TRANSMUTING EMOTIONS

Our ability to imbue chi or energy with a feeling or purpose is unique in creation. This purpose can be passionate or determined. The purpose can be to express joy or pain, happiness or sorrow, and more. All of this is possible at 5D. The difference is that you no longer need to dwell on any painful emotions; you simply notice them. You no longer need to continue to suffer for failures, pain, or loss. Instead you notice your emotions, and if they don't please you, you decide to abandon them. As you learn to observe and let go of painful emotions, you actually slip into joy, and become able to stay there for longer and longer periods of time. Joy comes from the complete dispersal of resistance and the mind being present in time (instead of out of time).

You are invited to look at your experiences as you look at colors. Is one color better than another? We think not. Do you have preferences for certain colors? Of course you do. Does that make them better? No! Having a preference for something is simply that, a preference.

Making Emotional Change

Choose self-love. Clear old outdated beliefs, and practice the mantra:
   Dear God, please show me how much I am loved.
Understand that everything is a choice. Claim your choice.
Replace darkness, anger, and frustration with validation: *I claim a day*
   of Heaven on Earth for myself and everyone I come in contact with.
Decide that everything is okay, even when you don't like it.
Decide that it's all good!
No making excuses.
Offer your opinion in this way: "This is my experience."

The "F" Word of Fifth Dimension—Flexibility

Look at table 5.1 (page 110) describing typical emotions from a 3D perspective and their 5D counterparts. See if you can actively choose 5D feelings once you notice your emotion.

What We Are Leaving Behind

Third dimension is a projection from other dimensions! The first time I heard this from my guides, I remember thinking, "Really?" They continued, "It is a projection from elsewhere." Think of a projector and a screen. Third dimension is the screen. The source is not the screen.

TABLE 5.1.
TYPICAL EMOTIONS IN 3D AND 5D

3D	5D
Patience	Compassionate indifference
Concern	Compassion
Judgment	Polite observation
Anger	Purposefulness and steadiness
Disappointment	Easy connection to other choices, other possibilities
Terror	Passive purposefulness, courage
Helplessness	Empowerment
Resentment Frustration	Acceptance—often to clear mass consciousness
Desperation	Abundance, awakening to fulfillment and plenty
Loss	Stepping into power (letting go of limiting beliefs may include releasing mass consciousness beliefs about life)
Feeling trapped	Freedom
Despair	Joy and playfulness
Heartsickness	Opening to *higher* expressions of love (planetary)
Shame	Self-worth and acceptance (healing karmic shame for self, family, ethnic group, and planet)
Longing	All longing is "missing God" and recognizing what it means to be on a planet and participating in a shift of consciousness, which claims new connections to the Creator
Feeling overwhelmed	New possibilities—breaking free of thought forms that control my life
Feeling violated	Expression of original intent and understanding that every experience will benefit life's journey

If all we see is what is on the screen, we might erroneously conclude that the screen is the source of reality. It is not. The third dimension is where we have been focused for thousands of years. It is the plane of existence from our current vantage point but is no more the center of the universe than the sun is.

If you find this confusing, the good news is that confusion is the temporary "new normal." In this state, many of you are detached from 3D but not fully under the magnetics of higher dimensions, which is why you may feel tired all the time. It also explains the extremes you may be experiencing emotionally. You will find that you are creating situations that will ferret out all that is not loving and kind within you. There may be someone who will benefit from your example and seek you out for advice. Do your best to let those situations come to you.

No matter how advanced you are, you may discover some minor occurrences will upset you—if so, let them go quickly. Know that this gift of becoming fifth dimensional gives you the bonus of creating instantly. It requires you to have a clear field, not because you have to clear your stuff in order to deserve or earn it, but because any bad thought could manifest just as quickly, and you need to be in the habit of only seeing the joyful version of any circumstance.

In fifth dimension you see life as a creation zone, as the environment where you get to choose what you want. Recognizing that you are choosing actually puts you into fifth dimension. This is good. Initially this may be driven by what you don't want, which is such a polarity statement that it will bounce you back into third dimension. That's okay—just make sure you move beyond "don't wants" into desires.

Sometimes you may not know what your "don't want" means, or you don't know how to get beyond it. Then your job is to simply ask for the "antidote" to your "not want list." (This is done by making a list of don't wants and then rewriting the list in the affirmative.) Leave the "how" up to the universe.

CLEARING YOUR EMOTIONAL BODY

Emotion is energy in motion. It is chi or energy that is qualified with a memory. However, it is energy that is caught in a web of time. Your emotional body represents the past to you. It stores the feelings of past occurrences. It remembers wounds and links to past wounds. It says, "This has happened before." And recognition sets in. It gives us the option to explore these experiences afterward. The problem is that the "captain's log" of emotion becomes a miasma of feeling that can be accessed, for some, too easily, replacing the present with its counterpart in the past.

Emotion must be felt to be cleared. This is why unexpressed emotion is so dangerous. Until we clear emotional wounds our Ascension process is limited. The Kabbalistic chant *"Kadosh, Kadosh"* given on my *Mantras for Ascension* CD, and the MerKaBa meditation given in chapter 10 are both ideal for clearing emotions.* They can help you heal your emotional body.

Lord Krishna† himself, star of the Bhagavad Gita,‡ has promised to deliver you from your emotional scars and hurts. He promises to help you with any childhood or other experience that is painful and difficult for you. Devotion to him is easy through singing mantras and bajans to him. According to Mark L. Prophet and Elizabeth Clare Prophet, in their book, *The Masters and Their Retreats,* Lord Krishna's request is to visualize him standing over any past wounds or traumas, in this lifetime or any others, while you pour out love to him through your devotional songs. He will take your love, multiply it, and pass it back through you to transmute that scene and that record.[1]

IF YOU ARE ALREADY A LIGHT WORKER

If you have become good at transmuting energy for yourself, or as a healer, you may be given additional burdens because you can move them

---

*See Suggested Resources for details on how to access this.
†Known as a Divine Being and an incarnation of the one true God, Krishna is part of one of the most celebrated epic stories—the *Mahabharata*—written between the fifth and second centuries BCE.
‡The Bhagavad Gita, required reading for many yoga instructors, is available on audio CD from Transformational Enterprises, Inc.

through you quickly. As a light worker, you probably have developed some of your gifts but may not realize you have even more power and gifts to give to humanity. Don't be discouraged. Instead, be like the weightlifter who easily helps someone with a heavy package! You need to see yourself as others see you, as someone who knows how to help. You are helping the Earth and humanity to heal, and it's your opportunity to express mastery at transmuting difficult energy.

If this is you and if you feel your burden is heavy, you may be carrying the weight of many on your shoulders. Don't do this as the path of least resistance. Do this with a glad heart. Decide this now. If there just doesn't seem to be any rhyme or reason for this weight, then you can accept you are carrying another's burden because you can. This is *not* "you with a burden"; this is "you with an opportunity of choice."

If the burden becomes too heavy, you are expected to ask for help from your angels and guides. This is the way of the free will zone. You ask for help, and it is given. Imagine your millions of helpers may wonder why you don't ask for their help! They hover close to you, knowing the big job you are doing. It's their job to help you when you ask. Ask often.

Allow this new belief system to move through you. It will open you up; it will expand not only your heart, your mastery, and your dimensional expression, but the energy for the planet as well. You become a fully active way-shower.

Many of you are here with so much light that you just need to "be." You don't need to "do" anything. If you have difficulty envisioning this, read about the life of Ramana Maharshi. You might be challenged with difficult thoughts but never have to actually experience difficult circumstances. Perhaps you are supported by others, family, inheritance, or trust fund. Everyone involved knows and agrees to this at some level. Great. You can stop feeling guilty about being supported! In the Akashic Records, many a seeker who has asked the question, "What did I come here to do?" has received as the answer, "You came here to be."

....

MANY OF YOU ARE HERE WITH SO MUCH LIGHT THAT YOU JUST NEED TO "BE." YOU DON'T NEED TO "DO" ANYTHING.

....

Handling Your New "Gifts"

Many of you will be able to feel the emotions of others. Initially, this might be mind boggling. You'll wonder why you are having so many varied feelings! Most likely it will be because you are either transmuting world emotions or feeling the emotions of someone you care about, without either of you realizing the other one is sending them your way!

A young engineer called me to ask about his strange emotional feelings. A few days after a relationship breakup, while he was doing laundry, he was able to discern that the emotions he had experienced a few nights earlier weren't his emotions. Until that point he had been thinking that the earlier set of emotions were his! Realizing that emotions that weren't his could still move through him, spontaneously and unexpectedly, was a shock.

As he explored his feelings, he began to see that he had been experiencing the emotions of his former sweetheart. This caught him completely by surprise. He also began to notice that he was putting up his own "antennae" to attract those emotions. Once he understood this was possible, and could explain it, he chose differently. So can you.

In another case, a woman was dealing with some heavy issues in her relationship, which were clearly related to her partner's failures. Yet she chose to work on forgiving herself! As she studied a Symbala (a form of sacred geometry developed by visionary artist Lahrinda Eileen), it literally transformed in front of her. Further, the feeling in the room transformed from grey and dullish to being full of beauty and color. She called me to ask, "Do you think I'm crazy?" Laughing, I said, "Nope, you've gone 5D just by using forgiveness on yourself!" What a concept!

Special Circumstances—World Service

I'm quite certain most of you have no desire to harm yourself. Yet in spite of this, some of you have found yourselves entertaining dark thoughts, being exhausted, and feeling sad and tired. Believe me when I tell you that you are not the only one feeling this and that you are transmuting for the planet.

Many of you are called to world service through your emotions. Thousands of light beings are having these difficult thoughts. None of them thought that it would include fatigue, failure, and loss. Yet as you shoulder these burdens and pick yourself up again, you will find you are filled with greater and greater strength. You are not alone. You must call upon your angels, guides, dragons,* and Ascended Masters to assist you. Just say it: *Dear God, Masters, Teachers, and all beings of one hundred percent God light, I need some help, and I need it now!* Say it over and over like a mantra—until things get better. There is so much darkness being released that when one light bearer is able to move past a dark thought he or she is carrying, that clears eons of misused energy; it clears humanity for future generations, thus making way for the Ascension!

---

*Dragons may be a new one for you! See chapter 11.

6
Language of Fifth Dimension

Louise Hay* awakened the world to the concept of our thoughts creating our reality. That was a profound shift toward beginning to understand how our thoughts birth reality. Louise taught us to be aware that our thoughts can create illness. She then taught that we could do something about our illness by changing our thoughts. She taught positive affirmations and has served as a world leader in the awareness of mind over matter. I consider her the leader of the positive affirmation movement. She first published almost forty years ago!

Now we are ready for the next level. As I began to formulate the ideas in this book, I started to recognize that there is a "language of fifth dimension." I began to notice word choices that I was naturally making as I spoke, ones that moved away from polarity. The other tip-off for me was that I found myself cringing when I heard others speak in ways that polarized them!

The language of 4D is all about emotions, which add a charge to

---

*Recently dubbed "the closest thing to a living saint" by the Australian media, Louise L. Hay is also known as one of the founders of the self-help movement. Her first book, *Heal Your Body*, was published in 1976, long before it was fashionable to discuss the connection between the mind and body. Revised and expanded in 1988, this bestselling book introduced Louise's concepts to people in thirty-three different countries and has been translated into twenty-five languages throughout the world.

our communications. Sometimes the charge is very polarity based, such as when, for example, you focus on "what terrible thing happened" or on remembering all the hurts and wounds you have had. To discover your own habits, all you have to do is intend to notice the way you speak of your experiences and how that colors your current situation. When you discover your own "source code," you can change it. Just like programmers spend hours finding a bug in a program, you can find the "faults" of your own conscious or subconscious actions and then do something about them. This book will help. There are also specialized healers that work on clearing trapped emotions, which cause a person to be sick or to remain stuck in ill health.*

• •

LANGUAGE IS A STRONG AND SIGNIFICANT KEY TO CREATING MORE MASTERY AT EVERY LEVEL. LET YOUR LANGUAGE BE OPEN ENDED, WITHOUT PREFERENCE OR PREJUDICE, SO YOU CAN SPEAK THE LANGUAGE OF FIFTH DIMENSION.

• •

WHY LEARN THE LANGUAGE OF FIFTH DIMENSION

You may not realize how much your language heavily impacts what is happening in your life. As you talk to yourself and others, what stories are you telling? What patterns are you reinforcing? Many are blind to how, through repetition, we empower the stories we think about and the stories we tell. That is why it is so important for you to learn how you can create and inhabit fifth dimension by consciously choosing your words.

---

*Recently, I've discovered the work of Dr. Bradley Nelson. I highly recommend his certified healers, who are available to help you with your own healing (they can be reached via www.ClearingEnergy.org).

To clarify, whatever you focus on strengthens your heart's desire and creates more of the same (what you authentically desire). Language is a strong and significant key to creating more mastery at every level. Let your language be open ended, without preference or prejudice, so you can speak the language of fifth dimension with grace and ease.

Some Specific Tips

To start with, notice your verb preferences and your verb tenses. Next, I invite you to stop using terms such as "weird," "hopefully," or "funniest thing," which imply unexpected (and not normal) results.

The word "strange" also has negative connotations that feel and sound destructive or damaging. Consider abandoning such common words and replacing them with words that have no charge. The following phrases will help you to do this:

- Happily, we are moving forward.
- That was so interesting.
- Joyfully we are moving into . . .
- Gratefully I'm experiencing . . .
- Delightfully I am . . .
- I'm happy to . . .

LEARN TO HELP YOUR MIND MOVE INTO THE EXPRESSION OF NON POLARITY, MAKING IT EASIER FOR YOU TO BE IN FIFTH DIMENSION. CHOOSING TO CHANGE THE WAY YOU SPEAK IS AN IMPORTANT AND NECESSARY STEP.

Avoiding Language That Locks You In

"I have to . . ." is probably the biggest offender among language habits that will keep you locked in 3D. You never "have to" anything. You always have a choice. You may not like the consequences; you may have cultural or family pressure to do certain things, yet there is always choice! Decide to banish that phrase from your speech and thoughts. It will help you sustain fifth dimension.

When you use a "have to" phrase, you empower anyone who seizes power over you. Deciding you no longer need to say "I have to" frees you. You don't "have to" pick up your daughter at 4 p.m. You choose to do so. Once you take ownership of your world, you create an irrepressible boundary around you. It means that no one can hurt you unless you "let" him or her. How do you let someone hurt you? You create a relationship, create expectations . . . and then they let you down!

What then are you to do when this happens? The answer is simple. You feel the hurt. You acknowledge the wound. You validate yourself by noticing your expectation (which creates the hurt) and disappointment (the emotional feeling from failed expectations). You own *both*. Then you love the other person anyway. Or you decide your relationship with him or her is over. Either way, you are in charge. You are the decider.

Another equally debilitating phrase is "I'd rather die (or eat ****) than clean toilets." The implication of the phrase is that you'd rather do something horrible or bad (like dying or eating something disgusting) than do a particular act. Just say you'd "rather not" and skip the colorful metaphor.

Avoiding these types of phrases really can condense to being more loving and accepting of yourself and others. You don't deny your emotions; instead, you validate them by giving them a voice—just three times and no more—then choose new words. Decide that duality is *not bad*, just a choice. We are choosing to become fifth dimensional, not because polarity is bad or wrong but because we have accomplished all that we set out to do in the polarity experiment and extremes are no longer desired.

. . . .

USING THE LANGUAGE OF 5D WILL OPEN YOU UP TO CHANGE YOUR PERCEPTION OF WHAT IS POSSIBLE.

. . . .

More about Empowering Words

DNA in living tissue has been proven to react to language, especially when combined with specific frequencies.[1] Limiting language has just as much of an effect on your DNA as language that empowers you. Listen closely to the words people use and to your own internal dialogue (that little voice in your head); see how often you use limiting language to determine what you can and can't do. Table 6.1 illustrates language choices that can either limit you or lead to empowerment.

TABLE 6.1. WORDS OF POWER TO REPLACE COMMON LANGUAGE

Common Language	Words of Power
I can't	I won't (yes, it's your choice—own it!)
I should	I choose
It's too difficult	I choose to make it fun and easy
It's not my fault	I think I'm responsible; how can I help fix it?
Challenges	Opportunities
Why me?	God must know something I don't know, because I know I only get things I can handle
It's a problem	It's an opportunity
It's too painful	I'm learning to cope
Life's a struggle	Life's an adventure
If only	Next time I'll choose differently
What will I do?	Just show up!

On Taking Offense

No one can insult you without your buy-in. Sometimes it is your beloved, whom you love and respect. You want him or her to be perfect—but he or she is not. Sometimes it is a relative or acquaintance. Wouldn't it be lovely if your family were always speaking what they really mean?

You might want them to be perfect; however, acceptance is your ideal response. In families, if it is your partner, you should speak up. In all cases, love them anyway.

....

ONCE YOU TAKE OWNERSHIP
OF YOUR WORLD, YOU CREATE AN
IRREPRESSIBLE BOUNDARY AROUND YOU.

....

MAKING THE CHANGE
PHRASE BY PHRASE

You can use table 6.2 to locate your "typical" ways of speaking—the words that you use most often. If you are using words shown on the left, take time to find new words to replace them with or try our suggestions shown on the right. This will help your mind move into the expression of nonpolarity, making it easier for you to be in fifth dimension. This choosing to change the way you speak is an important and necessary step. It means that you are consciously choosing thoughts that stay out of judgment and away from polarization (even statements like "I'll choose the right thing next time" imply polarity!).

Notice that when you decide to say, "I choose," or "I prefer" instead of "I can't," "I won't," or "I should," it invites both you and your listener to acknowledge your true power. In this way, you are officially announcing that you get it, that you have a choice, and you own that choice. This is officially fifth-dimensional talk.

This is another way to look at the "no more karma" issue. We are getting off the wheel of darkness and light and stepping into an existence that no longer requires darkness to see the light. The expansion of the earthly drama is over, and you are free to create the landscape of your choice on a clean slate.

TABLE 6.2. LEARN THE LANGUAGE OF FIFTH DIMENSION

Abandon these words of the third dimension	Use these words to stay in fifth dimension
I have to (being forced)	I choose, I prefer, it pleases me to
I won't, I can't, I should	I choose, I discover, I like
Betrayed	I experienced loss, now it's an opportunity to understand
Right	I champion your right to believe that, as long as it pleases you (implied: I claim my right to do the same)
Right vs. wrong	I see it as a choice
Wrong	This doesn't please me right now
Like, dislike, hate	Decide to like something in the present moment even if it's a new idea, match/no match
The truth is (whose truth??)	What works for me
Good	Cool, awesome, stunning, fabulous
Bad timing	Not yet, divine timing
Bad experience (anything)	Interesting experience
Better	Fascinating, interesting, inviting
Why? (narrow), Who did this?, How did this happen?, When did this happen?	I wonder? (open ended), What's going on? (open ended)
I don't know	It is useful to know, I choose to know, I choose to find out, I can look into that, I believe
Strange	Curious, fascinating, interesting, complex, wonderful
This is how it is	I've found that
Weird	Interesting, unusual, amazing
I don't understand	I choose to understand, I'll find out
Best/good	Juicy, attractive, noteworthy
Lessons	Opportunities

SWEAR WORDS

I recently encountered a fairly spiritual woman who used swear words, insisting that she was exercising her free will and was simply using the same words that everyone else does. She felt that the swear words are just words and didn't mean anything more than any other words. From a logic perspective, using that argument actually frees the other side of the discussion to surface. Many people use powerful swear words to create emphasis and to intensify their message and their emotion. Using those words emphasizes their cyclical nature.

For example, when you pray the rosary, you are tapping into the thousands of people who have prayed the rosary. As you repeat the same prayers, it causes you to be impacted by this greater energy of all the persons who have said the rosary. Likewise, using words that have traditionally held harsh, fierce meanings will pull in that energy. We must choose to be mindful of our choices—knowing that when we speak garbage we will attract garbage.

HOW YOU ASK QUESTIONS

Get in the habit of examining your questions! Much can be learned from writing the deepest questions of your heart in a journal. Get in the habit of noticing your questions. Do you ask so that you can assess a situation or compartmentalize it (such as as good or bad)? This is using your mind (mental body) alone. Once you decode whether something is good or bad, then you are compartmentalizing. This keeps you in third dimension.

In fifth dimension, nothing is either good or bad. Labeling people, events, and thoughts good or bad limits them. It confines them and puts them in a box that allows you to limit and classify them. Can you turn away from something without judging it? Think of something neutral like the colors of the rainbow. Is one color better than another? No. Some colors work better with others; some colors may harmonize with all colors in all circumstances. This is a good place to start.

Choice is the key to understanding fifth dimension. Choice is the version of reality that says you are no longer a victim—when you decide you don't "have to" anything. Understanding this guides you to ask certain kinds of questions in particular ways that don't reflect polarity. For example, instead of asking, "Why did this happen?" or "Who did this?" or "When did this happen?" you can ask "What's going on?" The questions based on "Who? When? Where? and Why?" are guaranteed to keep you in polarity. They do this by gathering information that allows you to compartmentalize the answer and solve it with your ego. Only the "What?" or "Wonder?" questions are open ended enough for you to get all the information. Amazingly, when you pay attention to how you ask, you may discover a whole lot more information that was just waiting to enter your consciousness!

When you use your heart to decide, you are honoring both your mind and your emotions. This allows you to validate your observations and choose wisely! When you plant yourself between polarities, by choosing good or bad, you are forcing yourself to stay in third dimension. In fifth dimension you might observe information as useful or not useful rather than good or bad.

Notice how you describe things. Do you say, "We are fixing a mistake"? Or can you say, "We are changing the way we do this"? In one version you are highlighting the error, thereby focusing energy on it. In the other, you are completely proactive, offering your crystal-clear intention to the universe.

And . . . forget dying to do anything! This is such a common phrase in American English today! Start living to do something. Change out your words, or at least change *this* one. Become eager to do something.

HIGHER SELF CONTACT

When you decide to ask the question "What's going on?" to discover information, you will see the easy unfolding of your fifth-dimensional self. Your angels and guides want you to use your Higher Self and cannot do it for you. Believe it or not, they don't always know! This is why your higher, fifth-dimensional self is so very important to this process.

When you learn to use your tools that help you *know* what you need to know, then you will always stay in fifth dimension. The most important tool is your heart. Your heart taps into your Higher Self with grace and ease.

Divination Tools

In general, divination tools like pendulums or muscle testing are useful because they help you get outside of your ego. But your pendulum can be wrong! And frankly it is not as useful as your Higher Self connection. Once you have this skill, you can discern whether you are acting or reacting in a third-dimensional way or in a fifth-dimensional way. Always, always, ask each and every day. Don't assume you know. When you assume you know the answer to something, you are in ego! Always check in with your Higher Self. It's an act of humility, which reflects in each moment that you are new, unique, and different. For this reason, you don't ask about actions for tomorrow that can wait until tomorrow to be decided.

Reason or Higher Self?—Why Not Both?

To understand how this process works, consider the following story. When my husband was courting me after meeting me at an event, he offered me a dream vacation to Hawaii. I was planning to return from Japan at the time of the trip, making the timing ideal. Yet I had only been talking to him over the phone for a few weeks and did not know him very well. We'd not actually gone on a date! His plan was for three months into the future. I did not think I should go—even though it was very tempting. I said to him, "I don't know you well enough to entertain such an offer!" But I "checked in" with my Higher Self, which said, "Go." I was so surprised.

So in this example, first I listened to the voice of reason, then I stepped back into my Higher Self before making the decision. If I had not voiced my objections first, I might have questioned my Higher Self's accuracy, or might have thought I was being swept away by his enthusiasm.

When you learn to use your Higher Self, you are becoming like a child in that you are willing to entertain all possibilities, even the frivolous and crazy ones! It also means you go through the process of logically thinking through the choices so that your mind is satisfied you've done due diligence.

Why go through the reasoning process if you are going to do what your Higher Self says? You do not have to listen to the voice of reason. However, there is great benefit in doing so. When you take the time to examine possibilities, or to do the research, you may discover that doing so yields information that you didn't know. Your research expands what your ego may know and helps you as a human to step into your power. Recognizing human data is very grounding. Even if you select an action not based on reason but on your Higher Self guidance, you are committing an act of will to be in your fifth-dimensional zone.

··

WHEN YOU LEARN TO USE YOUR HIGHER SELF, YOU ARE
BECOMING LIKE A CHILD IN THAT YOU ARE WILLING TO
ENTERTAIN ALL POSSIBILITIES, EVEN THE FRIVOLOUS AND
CRAZY ONES! IT ALSO MEANS YOU GO THROUGH THE
PROCESS OF LOGICALLY THINKING THROUGH THE
CHOICES SO THAT YOUR MIND IS SATISFIED THAT
YOU'VE DONE DUE DILIGENCE.

··

After listening to reason you are ready to make a decision because you have good options before you. You have satisfied the mind. When you question your Higher Self at this juncture, you are satisfying the ego-mind-heart marriage. The ego-mind has gotten you this far in life and into your spirituality. To ignore it now is almost impossible. Yet by using it to explore possibilities and then asking your Higher Self, you won't have the internal battle. Your ego will be heard, like a child who is persistent in asking questions. Once the Higher Self has been asked, the discussion is over. You never have to second guess or doubt yourself again. You can choose to follow your Higher Self.

Integration

Merging your ego with your Higher Self allows you to develop one will—God's will—within you. This work has never been done before, and you are charged with this mission. Are you up for it? If you will take the time to accomplish this one goal, no one, no teacher, no friend, nobody can ever deceive you again! You get to decide your actions based on the information that is valid in the moment. You may have noticed I didn't say "the truth." This is because there is no "truth." Truth is always circumstantial and involves the specific moment. In the moment you may know the truth of a situation—which certainly is valuable. But remember there is no "official" truth in fifth dimension. This is because truth implies its opposite—which doesn't exist in fifth dimension.

You can even "double blind" yourself by asking a friend to label one answer "A" and the other choice "B." You don't even know the answer when you ask your Higher Self. "Is it in my highest and best good to do A?" "Is it in my highest and best good to do B?" Just remember, when working with your Higher Self, be sure to always ask, "Higher Self, is it in my highest and best good to [fill in the blank]?" This is because you don't want any other energy to answer this question. You only want your Higher Self to answer.

7
The Time and Space Continuum

His car was moving too fast, losing control, leaving the road. My older brother woke up in a cold sweat before the collision. He didn't know it at the time, but he was in real time with my sister, Kathy, who died in a car crash—as described. I come from a large family. I was the middle child of six, and my younger brother, Kathy's twin, had a similar dream and abrupt wakeup. You cannot imagine how they must have felt when it registered that they had shared the experience of her death.

The sharing of a similar experience happened with me as well. The morning I called my mother to share the devastating news that my marriage of twenty-five years was ending, she told me that she had dreamt the night before that my father had had an affair. I was then able to gently tell her, "Mother, move that to my generation." She understood. I have had many shared experiences with her over my lifetime; we have a very good relationship.

Time is not what you think it is. Time is a construct. You can learn to work with time in the same way you can work with any idea. Time only serves as an aspect of consciousness that all agree on. Reality expands and contracts millions of times per second. Change occurs in milliseconds, yet you see only a small part of it because it is like a folded paper fan. Time is a matrix. Just as you see only the creased edges when paper is folded into zigzags to make a fan, you experience only a very narrow part of creation. Time is fluid. It is nested, spiraled, and convoluted in many ways. The past, present, and future are all happening and interacting simultaneously.

Time is linked to events, locations, and more. It's not visible because you have been programmed to only see the 3D projection. So your "on" is what you are programmed to see; the "off" position is where your Higher Self dwells. Each expansion and contraction allows you to change the reality of the next moment. Invite yourself to expand what you experience—shift your belief of what is possible. Shift your perception to expand to all that is holding your reality in place! Although you may not yet understand this, your actions in the present can alter past and future events. Your future events can alter the present and so on.

The mass consciousness agreement of third dimension uses time as a construct to order events and help the mind to organize and sequence it. In third dimension, we usually experience time as inflexible. This rigidity was useful to acquire certain skills and understandings. In fifth dimension, time is one of the many constructs that you can work with. This means that you can adjust time; you can go back in time to heal and change decisions where you now "know better." This is different from trying to figure out if your past actions were in third or fifth dimension, because the figuring out is an ego-based action, enabling the mind to label and compartmentalize.

Deciding to take action when you know your prior choices were less than ideal is an act of humility. You are now ready to change reality; it becomes a choice of heart because you now know better. Consider that the past, present, and future are all shifting and happening at the same time. Your actions in the present can alter past and future events. Think of the possibilities!

STRETCHING TIME

It is so very important to consciously unplug from the time matrix because time is one of the ways that mass consciousness pulls you into its programming. If you're not locked into time, then you cannot be pulled along with the masses. It is only when people agree to follow along with time that they are marching to the beat of someone else's drum.

Yet adhering to the time matrix is useful at times. It might be useful for a family holiday where everyone agrees to meet at a certain time and have a big event with all who are present there and then. On the other hand, schools, factories, and other similar environments were all created to encourage you to be a slave to time and to create a mass consciousness mentality to the point that you could not have your individuation. Many a person is made to feel less-than by not participating in the time-space continuum.

On Time, in Plenty of Time

My first real experience of stretching time dates back to 1995. I had been experimenting with time and space meditations and understood that I could alter time, although I hadn't actually put the practice or myself to the test. I was driving my son to catch a bus to O'Hare airport. His college's orientation was the day after his high school graduation. My son told me he had no intention of not partying on graduation night! My response was, "OK, it's your choice!"

On that particular morning, we both overslept! I woke up exactly when the Van Galder bus to O'Hare was scheduled to depart from a park-and-ride some thirty miles from our house! I rushed to my son's room, and we were in the van within minutes of waking up. I asked my son to help me hold the frequency of what I was about to do and he said, "Mom, you got me this far, I completely surrender my energy to your manifestation."

I invoked the collapse of time and space around us and demanded that we reemerge on time and in plenty of time for my son to catch his connection. We drove the distance, some thirty miles, and pulled on to the freeway exit just as the airport bus was leaving the pickup point to enter the freeway, heading to the next stop!

It was decision time. Should we drive the distance to Chicago from

Madison, Wisconsin? Should we try to follow the bus to the next stop? Even though I had never planned on making the 135-mile drive to O'Hare, I had responded to my inner guidance the previous day by filling up my van with gas. Yet I didn't want to spend my morning driving to Chicago and back and asked my guides if we could catch up.

When I "checked in," I received confirmation that we could catch up with the bus. Even though we were only a few minutes behind the bus, we couldn't seem to see it on the freeway. I checked in again, asking, "Where will the bus stop next?" and received the answer: Janesville. Awesome! I couldn't have listed all the possible cities between Madison and Chicago if I had wanted to, but it didn't matter because my Higher Self provided the answer.

People who have traveled with me know that I'm not great at directions. As we approached Janesville, my heart sank because there were three Janesville exits! I hadn't counted on that! I checked in with my Higher Self again and asked, "Which one?" My Higher Self advised, "The first one." I said out loud to my son, "We are to take the first exit." As we turned on to the exceptionally winding and long exit ramp, I added, "If this is correct—you should be able to see the bus on the exit ramp." "You're right. I can see it," came his excited response! We were able to keep it in sight as it turned left, then right, down a winding road a mile or so off the freeway and into the depot—not a typical off-freeway stop! My son took the bus to O'Hare and made his connections to D.C. that day. I had no energy for anxiousness or worry or fear or anger! I was focused and on purpose.

YOU CAN STRETCH TIME

Try this the next time you are in a rush and starting to "worry that you will be late."

1. As you notice that your focus is on the negative possibility, on what you don't want, change your thought to "I can arrive on time."

2. Use your imagination—don't look at the clock. Instead, see time compressing, expanding, and bending to serve your purposes.

3. Then, when you arrive at your destination, notice in your imagination that it was perfect timing. And don't look at the clock afterward either! Instead know you have created divine timing.

WHAT KEEPS YOU LOCKED IN TIME

I was originally told there are five things that mass consciousness does regularly that anchor you into the time-space continuum of 3D. The first four things are coffee in the morning, the news in the morning either via the newspaper or the television, the weather, and going to work at the same time. The fifth includes big sports events and other big televised events like the U.S. presidential debates or elections. You can probably think of other things that everyone "does."

What you don't realize is that when you participate in these rituals you are giving permission for the "company plan" to be downloaded to you! This means you are unconsciously subscribing to the mass consciousness programming. For example, in many cities there is a weekly newspaper that lands on your doorstep. You didn't ask for it, but you must choose to unsubscribe in order to not get it. It is assumed that you want it, unless you call the publisher and opt out.

Handle with Care!

Consider removing the TV from your home or at the minimum, removing it from the bedroom (yours and your children's). One of my early spiritual teachers saw an entity jump right out of the TV toward her! I know of other instances where people have been "pulled to the TV" energetically for no apparent reason. This tool, the TV, should be used with caution and not treated as a necessity.

Three Ways to Unplug

Here are three things you can do to unplug from the mass consciousness of humanity in order to avoid getting caught up in following the crowd without practicing discernment. These should also be done so your energy cannot be inadvertently or inattentively pulled into mass consciousness.

First, if you are a morning coffee drinker, consider changing your first action in the morning practice. If you can, give up the coffee habit completely. If you must have it, change it up and have a coffee once in a while in the afternoon, or choose to have it in the late morning. And refrain from statements such as, "I'm not good until I have my morning coffee."

Next, shake up your habit of watching, listening to, or reading news or weather, TV, newspaper, or Internet at regular times. Don't be part of the masses!

Finally, stop watching mass media events, whether sports or special events. Much is going on while you are tied into mass consciousness watching a football or soccer game.

Anytime we participate in the mass consciousness culture, we are giving our permission—our participation—to everything that is being done to hold us back. Isn't it time you decided where your "mass consciousness" participation shall go? What does this mean? There are energy levels for everything. When you put your attention into something, you subscribe energetically with your emotional energy (at whatever level, mild or passionate) to participate in the mass consciousness thought.

When you do things that are "expected," then a lot can slip by you. When you step outside of "what's expected," you create a different path of evolution. By unplugging from typical "mass consciousness" behaviors, you can begin to think for yourself with greater perception. This is huge. It allows you to change the timelines; you change reality and everything that has occurred in alternate realities.

The Positive Power of the Group Mind

There are many positive group consciousness actions that you can do collectively. Join with other groups who pray for the water. Those who join together for very specific powerful healing for the Earth and her people have changed reality. This is especially true for "prayer days" and other promoted mass consciousness events to help humanity and the planet.

In 1998, a Global Consciousness project began with over seventy researchers worldwide. In seeking to study the collective human response, they are already acknowledging the very real possibility that a specific intense response at a specific time has been recorded. Their mission (in part) from their website reads:

> The Global Consciousness Project (GCP) is an international effort involving researchers from several institutions and countries, designed to explore whether the construct of interconnected consciousness can be scientifically validated through objective measurement.[1]

The group mind can be used in other ways. During the Super Bowl, many individuals are in lockstep with the action, the game, and commercials. What kind of focus do you think that could bring?

It is also true that the grid workers, individuals who work in ceremony in groups or alone to shift and adjust the grids on and around the planet, known to me use those mass consciousness events to make changes and alter time. For example, it is a known fact that when Princess Diana died, there was a huge upsurge of sympathetic energy focused on her and her passing, to the point that the well-wishers who were saddened by this loss actually created what could be called the Princess Diana matrix, or the humanitarian matrix. That humanitarian energy is still running on the planet.

There are matrices for everything living and every energetic pattern. These matrices are the energetic blueprint of each living thing.

Some matrices are used to hold reality in place. The matrices are available to slip through, meaning that you can unhook from any that you choose to disengage from. This is a product of spiritual mastery, and no instruction could be given at this level. This reality is being projected from sixth dimension, where you go in the dreamtime. Those of mass consciousness need to unhook from the programming that has been thrust upon them as slaves of the state. Time has been used on people as a means of control, forcing people to belong to the status quo, meeting the demands of corporations that require cooperation around time and timing, which no longer serves anyone. It is the sense of "I have to go to work" that is driving this agenda. There is a subtle inner awareness that could lead you out of the time matrix and give you freedom to stretch time, compress it, and mold it for your needs instead of limiting you!

Collective Energy for Peace

Popular peace troubadour James Twyman recently traveled to Syria, where he held a prayer vigil for the Syrian people in which he was joined at the same time by people around the world. He says of this recent event in February 2016:

The Rainbow

As we drove to the overlook, someone on the bus said, "Look at the sky." We looked out the window and saw a brilliant rainbow that completely circled the sun. It felt like a sign of what was to come. In an hour millions of people would join us energetically, sending their light into the situation in Syria, without judgment. The rainbow meant we were not alone.

The Battle

Hours before we arrived a battle raged just beneath where we stood. Bombs exploded and guns fired at the bottom of the hill just beyond the security fence. It seemed that we were up against more than we anticipated, but then something incredible happened. It was as if the war stopped while we joined together as one. The battle simply ceased and remained that way through the entire meditation.

The Wolves

Over one hundred people from many spiritual paths sat in silence as you and so many others joined us. We held that space for fifteen minutes, and when I looked at the clock to end the silence, before I said a word, the sound of a single wolf howling just below us echoed through the air, then more until there were dozens of wolves that howled for exactly one minute, and then stopped. It was one of the most incredible things we ever heard.[2]

STEPPING OUT OF TIME

Consciousness is now reinventing itself. And it must be outside of time in order to achieve outcomes without bias. For example, when I was a teenager and I wanted to cook in my mother's kitchen, I deliberately waited until my mother was not in the house so that she wouldn't be over my shoulder telling me what to do or how to do it. I felt very strongly that I wanted to do it myself from the cookbook. The reinvention is not as important as the outcome is. This is one of the ways that we completely erase karma or transform a series of events in the blink of an eye.

Reinvention involves an "out of time occurrence" where you fold time and create a new lineage for yourself. Next you focus on the present that is based on this new lineage, knowing the difficult circumstances are but a faint memory, and they don't rule you. It allows you to look at your past and literally compartmentalize parts that no longer serve you so that they cannot hold you back. It also becomes your takeaway of the difficult circumstances instead of their leading or coloring everything that occurs after.

This reinvention also allows you to step back from heavy emotion that you really aren't engaging with anymore. It's like leaving the lights on in a room that you aren't using! Stepping out of time may be a difficult concept to learn, but you can unhook from the mass consciousness experience of time.

Training for Working with Time

Start with your intention. Next expand your belief and understanding of the folding of time as in the example of the folded paper fan. Once you accept these mental constructs, you can start to step out of time. Follow the suggestions below to reinforce your decision to access this ability. This knowledge has embedded in it the ability to fold time, and move beyond it. And it's not literal time anymore. It is about choosing wisely—going early, coming late, and changing up your schedule. Don't be part of the mass consciousness drama.

Stepping out of time takes practice and is a delightful, playful thing to do. You won't need to do it very often, but knowing how allows you to move into mastery at a time when it may be desirable. Practice these skills as often as you can, and move into a new pattern of existence that is not dependent on linear time. Decide that this is something you want to learn, and stop wearing a watch or frequently checking the time on your phone. These are commitments to step outside of the mass consciousness agreements about time.

If you are self-employed you have a lot more control over "time" than someone who has to show up at a specific hour. If this is you, consider practicing by tuning into "time to get up, time to take lunch, and so on" in a way that follows the energy rather than the clock. And if you work whenever you want, stop setting an alarm clock. Whether you work for yourself or not, you can stop counting the hours you "get sleep." This includes refraining from saying, "I only got six hours of sleep last night." Who cares? What if your six hours last night were complete? What if that's all you needed for that night?

Fifth Dimension Actions to Accelerate Your Ability to Move In and Out of the Time-Space Continuum

Choose to let go of the pattern of looking at your watch, clock, or phone to check the time.

Choose to not wear a watch!

Make a plan for your day or trip, but then be completely flexible about it.

Don't play the radio, because the announcer may tell you the time. Instead, make play lists on your listening device so the passage of time is not related to a specific album length.

Stop using an alarm clock to get yourself up in the morning. (If you need to wake up at a certain time, ask Archangel Michael or your guides to make sure that happens.)

I have been working with time almost all of my adult life. I didn't realize (at the time) others weren't doing the same. Yet I understood that it never served me to wear a watch regularly or to set an alarm clock. It was in the early 1990s that I decided to stop setting an alarm clock. This was a period of my life where I was traveling to at least forty-five different cities a year leading workshops or sacred journeys. I never missed a flight. On one occasion, I finished my corporate day job, was packed and ready to go for the weekend, and was working on my "resource" book, like a happy child with crayons! I suddenly looked up and it was almost 2 a.m.! I thought, "Oh wow, I have to catch a flight at 6 a.m.!" I quickly put everything away and asked Archangel Michael to wake me up on time and in plenty of time.

At 6 a.m. I sat upright in bed, looked at the clock, and refrained from saying the obvious to myself. Instead I wondered what was going on. I was out the door and at the airport in about thirty minutes. When I got to the clerk, she said, "Your flight was canceled; we have to rebook you." I queried when it had been canceled. "Last night; the plane didn't come in from Chicago—so it wasn't here this morning." I realized that, had I set an alarm, I would have had only a few hours sleep, for a canceled flight! I actually ended up with double the amount of sleep that night than would have been possible with an alarm!

Isn't it time for you to play with time?

WHAT IS TIME?

Time is a construct that you can manipulate. The first step is to believe it, and the second step is to be playful with it. One of the ways your experience with time alters is the idea that when you are early, it takes "less time" to complete something and when you are late, it takes more time. But why? The answer is in the thoughts you are likely projecting. When you are late, you keep thinking, "Oh, I'm going to be late." Your mind races into the future, where you *are* late, making up excuses, trying to assuage the individuals who may be affected by your lateness, and so on. What if you imagined you could temporarily "part the curtain" of the time construct, step out of it, and then step back into it at the appointed time? This is entirely doable.

Of course you should always check in with your Higher Self first, to confirm that doing so is the highest and best good for yourself and everyone who may be affected by your actions. This is staying in integrity. Why ask? Because you are third dimensional when you come up with the need to change the time matrix, and you might not know all that must be known without a Higher Self check-in.

Seek opportunities that seem to be timely and in sync with whatever you are doing. Act on them. I exercise the mantra: "On time, and in plenty of time." I add this statement anytime I'm feeling anxious about how I can complete a project in an allotted time. Archangel Michael continues to remind me of this when I get anxious about a self-imposed deadline!

TIME IN 5D

What's happening with time is that in 5D you are observing yourself before you are actually taking action in 3D. You cannot call it a prediction because it's already in the reality that you've observed a few seconds before your third-dimensional self can observe it. This has been shown in science experiments where a test subject registers a reaction before the action! (This was based on vision, where the "reaction" was measured and scored before the input picture was shown to the subject.) In 5D, you are so plugged in to your Higher Self that you might not notice your physical 3D self is slightly behind it in linear time.

Have you ever had the experience of being in a traffic accident and everything slows way down while you are able to observe each millisecond with clarity? How is that possible—if time is completely linear? How is it possible to feel "as if" time is in slow motion? Go back to that folded paper fan, the zigzag imagery. When this happens, you've slipped into the fold. The heightened awareness that comes from being in an accident of this type gives you the chance to change and observe your reactions. Even if this has never happened to you, you may know someone who has described it.

You can practice "slow motion," as if you could turn it on and off; soon enough you will find that you can. Use this wisely. Time, space, and perception are intertwined. When you take time to see that you have plenty of time, you actually stretch time. Can you imagine working on a project with someone who tells you they are worried there isn't enough time to finish it? Can you suggest that you both imagine that you somehow manage to get everything done on time and in plenty of time? Sometimes you might say you are not stretching time; you are stretching your experience of it. In essence it is the same.

MESSAGES FROM THE LORDS OF TIME

Because my knowledge on this subject has been closely guarded, I've been unwilling to talk about these matters, due to the possibility of misuse. However, I have recently been guided to share the messages of Ascended Masters who speak through me. In the following channeled message, the Lords of Time, vast cosmic beings surrounding the expression of the time-space continuum, clarify information about the time-space continuum.

Channeled Message from the Lords of Time, October 2015

We are the Lords of Time, ready to assist you to maximize your comprehension and your understanding of the time-space matrix energy. Next, the time-space matrix is a flat plane; however, fluid, it follows the terrain of the situations and circumstances and can be bent and molded.

Furthermore, you can sweep your debris or other unwanted experiences out of consciousness by simply folding time. [Imagine sand on a piece of paper, and then folding two edges together and tilting it into the garbage basket.] This is your first exercise. We're now ready for specific questions and concerns.

What Is the Time Matrix?

The time matrix is a web that contains node points and also connects those intersected node points with opportunities and portals. The time matrix is woven into your DNA and therefore unhooking is a way of being rather than a choice of being. This means you could choose to step out of the patterns that reinforce the time that is being forced on you and unhook from your need to always know the time, to know how much time you have, and so on, and instead allow timelessness to move through you, so you can feel opportunities and instructions coming from your inner wisdom that you otherwise would not hear, because you would ignore them, since you already know the time. Do you understand?

What Is the Energy Matrix?

The energy matrix is the field that allows the flow of chi to be captured and directed. There are many ways humans use the energy matrix. When they conduct themselves in integrity, they are in alignment with the energy matrix.

When they take good care of their bodies and follow the circadian rhythms they need to follow, they create a connection with the energy matrix. Time is not the culprit! Stop labeling historical experiences as the reason of any discomfort. For example, "I didn't take my pills this morning; therefore, I am unwell," or "My feet always swell when I travel across country." It is also possible to direct the energy matrix or to direct energy through the energy matrix with purposeful training of energy.

Message from Sanat Kumara and the Lords of Time

This message from Ascended Master Lord Sanat Kumara and the Lords of Time (channeled through Maureen) appeared in the 2016 Predictions issue of the *Sedona Journal of Emergence.*

Sanat Kumara and the Lords of Time spoke the following:

We wish to address jointly some issues that people are wondering quite a bit about and that have to do with other versions of you and other versions of you in other timelines.

While it is true that there are multiple versions of you and there are multiple timelines and there are multiple expressions, we wish to clean up the understanding of this. . . .

We say that you must understand that many multiple versions of you exist by your choices. As you make a decision, when you are faced with regret or remorse and you contemplate that (focus on it) with your emotion, you are actually creating another thread of another version of reality that allows the alternate decision to be played out.

Every decision has five possible choices: two below grade, two above grade, and one we will call the divine choice or the Higher Self choice. The two above grade and the Higher Self choice, or the top three are your best-case scenarios. When you face regret about a decision, perhaps you still made the best decision in the moment, but at the same time you still feel regret. This is like a woman who divorces and has children she's worried about; she is worried about the children being away from their father, and so on, so she actually creates with her emotion another version of reality where they stay together.

Now, what is important to understand is that [alternate version of herself] is funded by her emotion and by her commitment to the scenario. It is also funded by her partner [through] his shame, his regret, his remorse, all [these emotions] contribute to the existence of the alternate version of reality. And it will continue to be funded as long as those emotions are held. As the person works through those emotions, and comes to terms with the decisions they have made, they gradually withdraw funding of it, and it gradually dissolves without energy to sustain it. It's also true that multiple versions of every decision occur in this way. What is not true is that there are infinite alternative realities. So probable possibilities and possible possibilities are the norm.

Now, you may revisit circumstances and situations with an eye for discernment and an eye for dissolution. Timelines are collapsing. As you resolve these emotions of regret and so on, right before you finally let go, you have a moment of awareness, your mind would translate it into a big "what if" and you might even have a glimpse of where it would have taken you had you followed that path. At that moment there's a shudder, or a pull back with great will that unhooks you and releases your attachment and your energetic support of that version.

Now, because timelines are healing, you might not even remember a situation or a scenario as it is about to be fully merged in your own timeline, like a thread being brought back to its proper place, and you have a fleeting memory and a very conscious decision "I'm so glad I didn't go there*" and it's complete. So the unhooking of that energy causes it to fall back in alignment with who you are today.*

Forgetting

This is also why people are forgetting, and forgetting that they forgot. Sometimes they notice that they forgot, sometimes they remember, and don't notice that they had forgotten. What is useful to begin to understand is that people waking up in the moment might not remember that yesterday they were carrying a grudge and today they have none. Each and every individual is doing his or her own reset. There are layers of reset programming available, so that individuals can actually tap into grids in their dreamtime and receive resets that allow them to filter experiences in a way that allows them to unhook from the trauma and the drama. Every effort is being made to release people from trauma and drama and to minimize the shock that might be felt when this knowledge starts to become visible on a wide scale.

EVERY EFFORT IS BEING MADE TO RELEASE PEOPLE FROM TRAUMA AND DRAMA AND TO MINIMIZE THE SHOCK THAT MIGHT BE FELT WHEN THIS KNOWLEDGE STARTS TO BECOME VISIBLE ON A WIDE SCALE.

We are not suggesting that people become desensitized as much as we are suggesting that people's humanity changes in a way that allows them to not need to desensitize but to be open, aware, and allowing, which is why they need upgrades to prevent them locking down into fear consciousness.

There are those that seek answers to the future. And we say to you with absolute certainty that the future is still uncertain—not in a way that might make you fearful, but in a way that says that we require you to decide your future. We require you to participate in the remaking of this free will zone, because you are in the middle of the free will zone while the remaking is occurring. This means when you encounter difficulty, or trauma or drama, you must begin to use phraseologies that are fun and release you from attachments.

So we will play with you and will say, many of you have heard the phrase, "Oh, I don't know why I didn't remember that, it must be a senior moment" and we say, no, it was a multidimensional moment! When you say this instead of the first statement, you claim your multidimensionality, you unhook from the mass consciousness, and you reclaim your authority to create your reality. When you encounter an obstacle that terrifies you— whether it is a bill you cannot pay or an angry situation that feels difficult to resolve, take a half a step back and say "there is a solution here and I am looking to discover it right away," or "I wonder what the solution is here." In this way, you are opening the pathways to solutions that you have not thought of. One encounters these difficulties and it is incumbent to look those difficulties in the eye and say,

> You have no power,
> You have no power,
> You have no power.
> There is a solution here and I demand that it is brought forth.
> Amen.

You name the outcome that you wish, and the universe will provide the solution. The universe has been created in such a way that it responds to the human. And the reason it responds to the human is because the human is carrying God DNA; God DNA is Creator energy. So whether people realize it or not, they have the power to command that does not exist anywhere else. This is why so many other races in the cosmos seek to work with you, to interact with you, to observe you, and so on.

Knowing that you have the absolute authority to command is very, very powerful. When things go wrong or awry or things happen that you find uncomfortable or displeasing, to know that you can have that experience and then allow yourself to say "But there's a solution here and I just have to discover it, or there is a solution here and I expect that I'll know the answer pretty quickly." This does not mean you do not take steps to protect yourself and so on, but at the same time, we want you to understand that there is no need to suffer anymore. This is the end of suffering.

• •

AS YOU LOOK AT THE COMING YEAR FOR OPPORTUNITIES,
EVOLUTIONARY SHIFTS, AND TRANSFORMATION AND MORE,
ONE OF THE THINGS THAT YOU CAN COUNT ON IS
THE END OF SUFFERING.

• •

As you look at the coming year for opportunities, evolutionary shifts, transformation, and more, one of the things that you can count on is the end of suffering. Humanity will no longer be able to create suffering for another. In addition, authority is waning. Those who have clarity and integrity will be stationed throughout the globe to continue to question authority and to question activities that impact humanity.

Misuse of power will no longer be able to be carried out. The example of the overthrow of Mubarak, Egypt's long-standing president, is your prime example. He, the head of Egypt, told the military to stop the riots and fire upon the people of Egypt, and the military refused—they would not use force to kill their own people. At every level there was, what we will call, civil disobedience. So part of what you will see more and more is the willingness for individuals to join with others to stand up for their rights as human beings and their rights as citizens.

Finally, you will see a shift, an even greater shift, we will say, because it's already in place, where people will no longer rely on what used to be called mainstream news. And they will come to conclude that their news is better from their friends, from blogs, and all kinds of alternative resources. We are ready for questions.

Question and Answer

In the following section you will see questions posed by me and answered by the Lords of Time.

Humans are so used to their traumatic experiences or identities, some are addicted to the experience of victimization or other by-products of trauma, and then we're a little off-put by the absence of that information. How or with what do we fill these released memories or resolved timelines so we do not addictively or habitually reinvent new traumatic experiences and bad feelings?

Well there's two things going on: First, there is an energetic residual. That's the first thing. And then the second thing is that it's the energetic residual that is causing you to go back into it. And there are those situations where, at higher levels of consciousness, forgetting has not kicked in and the subconscious is seeking to relay the event with a better outcome. So you create an experience, with the idea that you're going to get a different outcome. And you create it with different people and different situations, but you create the same experience to reassure yourself you didn't make a bad decision in the first place.

And we say to you, it isn't whether or not you made a good decision or a bad decision, it simply is an experience and you can decide at any moment, "You know what? I don't need that experience anymore. I don't need to go through that anymore." And to announce to the universe, "You know what? I don't need to do that anymore." The experience of, let us say, the woman who marries someone who beats her. Then she meets someone else and marries him and he beats her. She keeps trying to be happily married to someone who used to beat her and doesn't anymore—someone who has met her and is so in love with her that he decides to change. So she subconsciously is looking to create the experience and resolve it amicably. And we say it is possible and preferable at this juncture of history to let go of the need to create a replay to get a better outcome. Those opportunities are fading. This is why the forgetting is so important. This is why the forgetting can be so powerful.

Now, let us go back to, we will call it, the need or the desire to create a better outcome with the same scenario. And wouldn't it be lovely to step into a place where a human would have an experience and go, "Wow, that really was tough and I don't ever want to do that again." And you hear people say things like this. And this literally unhooks them from ever having to do that again.

Now we still want to go back and answer one more question that you raised and that has to do with, we will call it, the void, or the vacancy of, "what do I do now?" And we say to you, when you notice that you're in a scenario when you're about to repeat or about to replay some old drama with a new person, and you think to yourself, "I don't even know why I think that, I don't even know why I have that awareness, but I choose to unhook right here and right now." In fact, as an individual, you could say that prayer every day, for a little while, when you know you're forgetting and you're choosing to unhook, and say "I choose to unhook from any trauma or drama patterns that I may have enjoyed, that I may have encountered, that I may have explored. And instead, I choose to be part of the New Earth and the new experiences of creativity, and mastery and unconditional love and humanity."

We say to you, the Earth is a proving ground par excellence. There is nothing that you cannot do. It does not mean you can do everything today. It means that anything you seek to achieve with passion, you will do so. We say this to you with absolute certainty, absolute passion, and absolute clarity: seek that which makes you happy. Find everything that makes you happy, so that when you are faced with those voids, then the filling it becomes more of habit than of choice, decide that a new habit is appropriate. And that new habit may be something as simple as looking at flowers, learning the flowers' names, watching a sunset, so that you can replace those drag down emotions with your joy. As you continue to find joy wherever you are, joy will continue to find you. What else?

. . . .

WE SAY TO YOU, THE EARTH IS A PROVING GROUND
PAR EXCELLENCE. THERE IS NOTHING THAT YOU CANNOT DO.
IT DOES NOT MEAN YOU CAN DO EVERYTHING TODAY.
IT MEANS THAT ANYTHING YOU SEEK TO ACHIEVE
WITH PASSION, YOU WILL DO SO.

. . . .

Timelines are collapsing and converging—to what?

What we're talking about is creating multiple versions of reality. People who have large amounts of regret, and so on are creating alternate versions of reality.

We will play with you and give you an example. You go into the ice cream shop, and you want to have an ice cream cone, and you look at all the flavors and you really want chocolate. And then you remember you've got your favorite white dress on and if you spill a drop on it it's going to make you look funky. So you opt for mint instead, because you figure you're not as likely to drop it and even if you do you should be able to get it out, or maybe even vanilla because you want to be on the safe side. All those versions of reality now exist: one with you choosing mint, one with you choosing chocolate, and one you're experiencing in the moment with you choosing vanilla. Now we say to you that you have set those in motion by considering the possibility in the moment. These are harmless enough, but what happens is that there is a version of you that gets the chocolate, spills it on herself, then struggles about how to clean it up, then goes into a store and buys a great dress and is thrilled because she got this great dress that she never would have found otherwise. There's another version of you that spills the mint and cleans it up with not too much hassle. And the third version, the vanilla that doesn't even spill, not even a problem. And we say to you all those versions exist until they're no longer needed.

When you break up with a beloved, you create an alternate version where you didn't break up. That alternate version is funded by, perhaps, the partner who did not want to break up, and that is energetically supported by both of you as you work through your guilt, your regret, and so on. Those alternate versions are threads of you that are going to collapse and move back into your mainstream.

So, for example, we will give you the example of resolution. The resolution is you getting chocolate all over yourself, and then getting a different dress, and thinking, "wow, this dress was on sale, I would never have seen it in this particular neighborhood, blah, blah, blah"—it's a happy resolution and the whole episode is resolved and reintegrated in you.

Another version is where you struggle.

And the other version is where you don't get exactly what you want, but you don't struggle.

And each one of those gets integrated back into the present. So you do take more than one path. You do take both paths. As Frost would say, "The road less traveled or the road not taken?" And we would say, "Well, they're all *taken!*" by you!

For a time . . .

For a cycle.

8
Finding Your Fifth Dimension Way

Becoming fifth dimensional is different from anything you have done before. In this, your intention is paramount. You cannot move into this realm without an act of will. Of course, once you start to inquire and explore, you then have enough information to use your will to ask for assistance in becoming fifth dimensional. I recommend you ask every day.

You have a responsibility to be completely honest with yourself. This is hard. It's often referred to as shadow work. It means you ask your friends to tell you the truth. It means you accept every criticism with a "thank you" and a firm resolve to get to the bottom of the complaint! It means you love yourself anyway, imperfections and all. It means you are willing to change. It means you don't need to defend. Instead, you decide to learn from your critics and that you are finished with lying and all the shades of grey. Doing this also reinforces your unconditional love commitment to yourself!

ETHICS WITH UNDERSTANDING

You cannot be in fifth dimension without ethics. At the same time, you really don't need ethics in 5D, because you won't have any motivation to misbehave there. This is because in fifth dimension the not-God choice doesn't exist. What are ethics anyway? Having ethics is a willingness to allow your words, thoughts, and actions to be in alignment, to carry the same message. While you are vacillating between dimensions, ethics are a handy concept to adopt, to help you stabilize who you really are.

When you decide to do the "right" thing because you may get caught—that's moving in the direction of fifth dimension, but it's *not* taking you into fifth dimension. When you choose to practice ethics (because of a standard instead of fear of getting caught), this practice moves you into fifth dimension. Deciding and taking action to practice ethics will put you in 5D. You will stay in 5D when your thought, word, and action are in agreement. Making sure that what you say, think, and do all "line up" and are in agreement keeps you fifth dimensional. Deciding you want to do something without external motivation is the joy choice.

In fifth dimension, you care about your neighbor or the other person as much as you care about yourself. When you create relationships, partnerships, or friendships you move to a place of deep compassion that is above reproach. Although we are explaining this in third-dimensional terms, in truth, the idea of taking advantage or getting the better hand is not part of your thought process in fifth dimension, as that ceases to be a motivator. Instead, you are motivated by cooperation, fairness, and friendliness. Whew!

You may ask, "But if I don't look after myself—who will? If I don't make sure I'm safe, how can I do what I came here for?" This is that old paradigm coming down again. Choosing to look out for the other person the same as you do for yourself insures that you only attract and will partner with like-minded individuals. Certainly this may take trust to start with. Trust me (pun intended) when I say you *know* that you are partnering with like-minded individuals; this ceases to be an issue. I am not suggesting you avoid taking care of yourself while taking care of the other. Instead, the "caring" is simultaneous and mutual.

One of the primary signals of fifth dimension is this wonderful energy of caring as much for others as ourselves. This also can be learned and adopted. Why not? It improves your life and guarantees that you are also helping at least one other person. Think of the changes in our world if every exchange of any kind involved both parties looking after the welfare of each other.

This does not make you a benevolent king who decides what the other person needs. Instead you ask him, "Are you satisfied? Did you get what you wanted?" Impressive. Who can you have that kind of exchange with now? Could you practice with him? Could you try it out with someone?

Modern man has been inclined to compete with his perceived rival. Yet if we all participate in the raising of the standard, everyone benefits. It needs to start somewhere. You don't need me to tell you to act as if everyone is watching—but that's your key. Behaving as if everyone is watching will help you to develop an intensified sensitivity to integrity. What you used to think of as acceptable or okay will shift, change, and improve with time.

BEHAVING AS IF EVERYONE IS WATCHING WILL HELP YOU
TO DEVELOP AN INTENSIFIED SENSITIVITY TO INTEGRITY.
WHAT YOU USED TO THINK OF AS ACCEPTABLE OR OKAY
WILL SHIFT, CHANGE, AND IMPROVE WITH TIME.

PRACTICE REJECTION
WHEN THERE ISN'T A MATCH

Get comfortable with rejecting anything that isn't a match for you or doesn't match who you are. You don't have to make the person or situation bad or wrong—it's simply "not a match" for you. Don't make it about her—instead, tell her, "I champion your right to do or think this, even though I won't."

Let's begin with how you normally exist. You are typically monitoring what is going on and alternately participating in controlling the situation and circumstances. What if you could consciously move to a place of only noticing, without action or reaction? If you can do this, you will give yourself space to learn whether what's going on is a match for you. You might be tempted to judge a situation or to compartmentalize situations or people a certain way, but noticing without any reaction or control allows you to decide whether something is a match for you.

This may seem like a subtle difference, but it is important to understand the distinction. Match/no-match is a nonpejorative, nonjudgmental way of experiencing versions of reality without engaging. It is very powerful. It allows you to move from 3D into 5D, while still engaging in third dimensionality. You've now become multidimensional!

Here's how self-observation works. When you notice you are paying attention to something, pull back slightly, and notice your feelings around it. As long as you are engaged in monitoring it, you are controlling it. With a little self-awareness, you can start to unhook from controlling it and move to simply noticing it. Then you are ready to

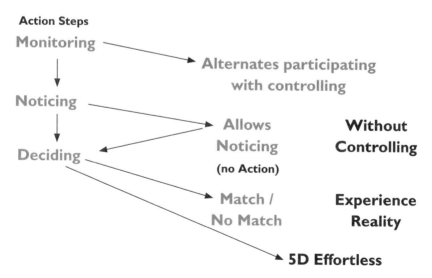

Figure 8.1 Monitoring diagram—if
you are monitoring it . . . you are controlling it

observe whether it is a match for you! If you mentally begin to engage in "reactionary" feelings or thoughts, you've moved back into control mode. If you are able to notice your feelings and thoughts, and then allow yourself to decide whether they're a match, that enables you to stay in 5D without engaging in 3D reactions! This is a very powerful mode of being.

When you get to the deciding phase, and you're examining the situation as either a match or not, that effortless decision anchors you at 5D.

Motives and Judgment

Examine your motives. When you are questioned about your behavior, don't immediately dive into explanation; instead seek to understand yourself and your motives. You may discover you are not where you thought you would be.

Learn to practice discernment—not judgment—so you won't compartmentalize things into good or bad; instead it's a match or no-match for you.

THE WAY-SHOWERS

The way-showers are leaders or knowers, and they are all around you. This term first came to my attention almost twenty years ago through a client reading, when the Akashic Records guides told my client that she was one of the way-showers. The way-showers lead by exposing the truth and bringing it to the eyes of the public, where many can benefit from this knowledge. The role of the way-shower is not to say, "Follow me!" The way-shower encourages all to use their gifts and be their best selves. They say, in effect, "Do not believe me—ask your inner guidance." This is the teacher you can trust. Any teacher who teaches you to follow them—and then expects you to only follow—is still in ego and is *not* trustworthy.

A way-shower may be well read, or a meditator, channel, guide, or just a very spiritual being who has come into embodiment on the Earth in order to help souls find their way. There are way-showers, and there are Masters. Sometimes the Masters are pushing the buttons of the way-showers. This is to push the way-showers into their own Mastery! Yet all are working together for one purpose, to collectively become 5D.

Seek teachers that invite you to challenge them and ask you to prove their teachings for yourself. This doesn't mean you openly ridicule or deride the teacher, but that you take the teaching that is given and explore it within yourself. Then ask, "Does this work for me? Is this in my highest and best good? Is this the truth I seek?" There can be highly acclaimed teachers who will falsely teach you. Your responsibility is to discern the difference and honor your inner wisdom.

THE GUARDIANS

If you are a guardian, you are a protector and companion to very high souls who have important work to do. Your job is to just show up and be a guardian for the new teachers. You "look after" other sacred souls who are helping to pave the way for the new family of humanity. You don't have to "do" anything—yet your job is just as important. I have had many guardians in my world. You do not have to go through the same machinations everyone else does. Your life is smooth, uneventful. Living is productive and abundant, yet you don't have a particular ambition, goals, or requirements—except to show up.

ALL RIGHT—BUT WHAT DO
I HAVE TO GIVE UP?

In a discussion I held years ago, a man said he wasn't willing to give up certain aspects of this 3D life, such as food. I nodded in agreement and said, "I know what you mean, but try to think in a bigger way. Think of how much you have changed since you were a child. For example, a six-year-old's favorite restaurant might be one of the many fast-food restaurants. When this child becomes an adult, he would never dream of impressing his sweetheart at a fast-food restaurant. Instead he knows the pleasures of fine dining."

You will be pleased when you have recreated your reality that represents the desires and possibilities of a 5D being. As we evolve and let go of the pleasures that we currently are attracted to and enjoy, we will discover far richer, more meaningful, and more enjoyable experiences and structures that will provide greater satisfaction for others and ourselves. This part is important. One of the changes you will be experiencing is not being satisfied unless the other is too.

So what will you give up? Unhealthy habits. Pay attention to the foods you consume and use organic versions whenever possible. You'll know when and if you are ready for a healthier diet.

MERGING LIFETIMES

Many of you are abruptly and unexpectedly experiencing past lifetimes that may have ended horribly. You're revisiting them and having experiences that replicate a particularly difficult experience. Well-known author and physician Norm Shealy told me of a number of times where he experienced himself being choked to death in a dream. When he figured out who he had been in a past life, then the nightmares stopped. Other experiences aren't always so easily resolved.

Fear can carry over from lifetime to lifetime and keep us locked in a place of powerlessness. Once you have knowledge—you are free. The important thing here is that it is easier to step into your divinity once you have these realizations. The timelines are merging to build a new reality that isn't filled with so many missteps.

Initially the transition from 3D to 5D can be so humorous that you have to laugh. You finally realize the things that were life and death sometimes aren't. And you discover the person or thing that you were most afraid of—the thing you have most been in a stranglehold over—is simply your belief about it, and you can actually playfully say, "Poof! You're gone!" and watch the person or thing lose power over you.

OTHER VERSIONS OF YOU

In my practice, I sometimes meet two similar people for readings around the same time. This has happened multiple times, with two individuals of uncommon names showing up on the same day. They either purchased an Akashic Records reading, registered for a class, or came to the same workshop on the same day.

One time at my office we thought we were dealing with one Carolina, whom I already knew. Only weeks later did we discover that the Carolina we had been speaking with was a new and different woman who was also asking for an appointment with me. They had both scheduled a private session with me for the same day. At first, we couldn't understand how they had gotten so turned around in our minds. But the circumstances were so peculiar and synchronistic that when I asked what was going on, the answer was the "obvious"—they are the same soul!

Next I asked, "Should I say something?" My Higher Self gave a big "yes," and I introduced them to each other. One lived in Florida. The other was moving there the following week!

My files are filled with individuals I meet worldwide that are the same soul. They often are working through different aspects of the same topic. It's always a delight to work with them, and—with my Higher Self's guidance—I'm able to know if it is in everyone's highest and best good.

The Adams

I've come to the conclusion that there are several versions of everybody. What's the benefit of meeting or knowing another version of you? You might work together, maybe even help one another achieve something not possible to do on one's own.

Here's an example of the many versions of one soul: a group of men I knew through various friends who knew each other well, and some even attended my classes. How did I know they were all the same soul? Many "hints" came in, and when I checked in with my

TABLE 8.1. FOUR VERSIONS OF ONE SOUL

Qualities	Life 1	Life 2	Life 3	Life 4
Names changed but representative. Notice three have the same first letter (a vowel). Notice two are the same except for one vowel.	Adam	David	Adum	Allan
Profession and interest	Medic in WW II, engineer/farmer/very spiritual, very family oriented	Engineer/spiritual, worked for the navy in engineering role, very family oriented	Engineer, medical doctor, very family oriented	Very mechanical, very religious, very family oriented
Birth date (excluding year)	Same date	Unknown	Same date	Unavailable
Ages	Now deceased	60s	50s	30s
Location	Same city	Same city	Interviewed for a job same city and decided not to take it; lived near me for a time	Lived near me for a time
All same gender	M	M	M	M
Race	White	White	Black	White

Higher Self, the "same soul" was confirmed. I'm leaving out some details to protect their identities. In one case, one man's face was superimposed upon the other, allowing me to clearly see both versions of the same man! Imagine seeing that!

This group of men is all one soul. I've met four of them. The first of them that I knew has been out of embodiment for about twenty years. When I met a younger version of him, Doug, they were both living in the same city. Both had chosen to live there. When I met the third one, I asked him if he was ever contemplating moving there. He said "yes" but then passed on it after a job interview. The youngest one is still discovering who he is. All of them were engineering types. One engineered inventions without any formal training. The next two had undergraduate engineering degrees. The first one and third one shared the same first name with one vowel change, the same birth date (not year), and had a strong connection to medicine. The first one was a medic in World War II and wanted to become a doctor. The second one became a medical doctor.

Notice the dramatic similarities in the chart to see the resemblances of one soul embodied into several generations, who crossed my path and interacted with me on a longer term. These are the embodiments that I met and knew personally. Obviously this person has an important and powerful influence in my life—which is why they showed up. These are some of his embodiments. I only know of this group of four—yet I would expect there are more out there.

This was a remarkable experience for me, as each time I met one of them, their identity had been spontaneously revealed to me without my asking. Was it always the same person? Yes. This "identity" of the "same soul" has come up over and over with many individuals. This mystery continues to unfold. Amazingly, it is occurring frequently—so much so that I know you may be having similar experiences.

Tapping into Another Version of You

Why is this important? Your soul can occupy two bodies. There is more than one version of you. This turns the whole belief in one soul, one body, upside down! What else do you believe that may not be true? It's time to expand your concept of reality. If you are honest with yourself you must accept there is more going on than you could possibly imagine from a linear perspective. You need to reconsider everything you thought about yourself, your life, your mission, and so on. You have the opportunity to become your most advanced self by changing the way you think about things. At least consider the possibility of being more open to other views.

As you begin to accept this knowledge of multiple dimensions and multiple versions of you, you can start to grapple with the mind-opening awareness that there is far more going on than you realize. Many of you may have heard this from other teachers. Perhaps it didn't really sink in. This may even cause you confusion. Find an anchor point in one experience that helps you validate this knowing. Perhaps you've had a dream when you see yourself on the "road not taken." Perhaps your meditations have given you insights to aspects of your life that you know are not the current life you live. Then remind yourself that you are expanding your focus, even as you remain in the ever-present now.

Imagine that you are swimming in the ocean. Looking at the shore, you might need two markers to get a sense of where you really are. As you get to "feel" what it is like to be in other dimensions, like a swimmer in the ocean, you can use markers that show up, and gradually you will know and identify. As you recognize that one version of reality is not all that there is, your perception increases. Sometimes your perception increases before you accept multiple realities. In order to get where you want to go, it is useful to respect your current position while keeping an eye on other positions, along with your future position relative to some outside marker. Be open to how that might occur! It's a bit like driving—you are aware of your position in traffic—and many other drivers as well.

Q & A with Maureen J. St. Germain

QUESTION: Although my breakup occurred six months ago, I still frequently experience strong emotional waves of anger, guilt, self-blame, betrayal, shame, and confusion. Cognitively, I am at peace with my decision of leaving this man, yet these emotions, including memories of arguments, and even *new* arguments that I would have "in my head" with him made me curious as to what is taking place.

MAUREEN: What is going on? First of all, you are not alone. There is another version of you who took the path of remaining with that partner. This situation you are experiencing with such strong emotions is a way for you to reach this other version of you still in the relationship. In fact, there are very likely five expressions of you: two above grade, two below grade, and one manifesting the Divine. Depending on how devoted you are to practices that help you hold higher vibrations, you can maintain different ones.

Q: How is the bleed-through possible?

MJS: The emotions are intense (emotional, visual in your memory, and sometimes even "hearing" or reliving the arguments in your head) and the contrast of those emotions is huge. Now, if you consider these big energy emotions, bearing in mind that the emotions are the bridge of the fourth dimension, you're using the 4D bridge to cross over to that version of yourself, meaning the two versions of you meet through this bridge.

Q: How do I deal with it?

MJS: 1. Notice that the other version of you is there and the emotions are real.

2. Look upon it/them as an observer.

3. Pull back enough to notice and say, "Ah, I'm having a feeling from another timeframe, from another version of me."

4. Look with compassion and say, "I'm so glad I chose *this* version [*my* version] of reality."

5. Know that you and others are funding the alternate realities with you. For example, you have concern for your ex-partner's welfare, and the guilt for his wound. Your ex-partner may be missing you, wishing you were still there.

6. Recognize that "funding it" means you're allowed to fund other realities. However, you can unhook from that sense of responsibility and guilt and say, "Everyone did their best including me,"

and then, ever so slightly, dismiss it. Dismiss it the way you would a child when you look down and say, "You good?" After the child says, "Yes" you simply say, "Good."

7. Just noticing that you're doing this is an opportunity to be okay with the emotions with which your ex-partner is funding that reality as well. Choice moves through this: As you stop funding this reality, he will no longer be able to do so. [That reality will cease to exist.]

8. Remember, this is all a game, and all the players are playing of their own free will. Don't feel guilty for your decisions, good or bad, and this will allow for ease.

Q: I was advised to write a letter to each and every person I have ever been angry with in my life and then ceremonially burn the letters. I found this procedure arduous. Is there another way to transmute anger?

MJS: That type of exercise is primarily for those who do not have the capacity for forgiveness, whose hearts are not sufficiently open to forgive to the extent that no one can do them harm. Simply use the ancient Hawaiian mantra practice known as Ho'oponopono: *I'm sorry, please forgive me, I love you, thank you,* and this will transmute through heartfelt forgiveness.

Another immediate method is through using the Kabbalistic chant *"Kadosh, Kadosh"* given on my *Mantras for Ascension* CD.*

DEALING WITH EGO

Our understanding of the ego in 3D is limited in scope; we've not understood the ego's need to survive. In the East, the ego is subdued, but there, people are not encouraged to be different in the individualistic way that utilizes the ego! In the West, our egos are far too "out

---

*See Suggested Resources for details.

there"—too big—to subdue. Better to teach the ego what is needed to transition and merge with 5D. Furthermore, "those who would have us fail" want you to believe that you have to use your ego to solve issues, to solve yours or someone else's problem.

In a recent blog post, I wrote about having ordered a few surprise presents for my cherished husband for Christmas, which were to arrive while I was traveling. I told him several days before I left that I had ordered a few things online. "Please do not open any packages that come while I'm gone." I knew he had *not* ordered anything so there was no need to tell him to look at the address label! I also texted him after I left with the same reminder (since he often opens everything that lands on our doorstep). I even sent an e-mail reminder too!

On my first day away, my husband reported to me that he put an intercom that came for me in my office! This was one of my surprise gifts for him. I was so upset. I was so hurt. Couldn't he even honor a simple request? He, on the other hand, could not comprehend my disappointment and agitation! I said, "Well, go ahead and try it out, and if you don't like it, we can put it back in the box it came in, and send it right back!" "Uh, actually, I threw away the outer packaging already."

I struggled with my frustration, asking in meditation, "What was going on?" The answer came in an instant! It was my ego! My "me" wanted to do something special for him—he does so much for me. I wanted to have something that he didn't already know about (he usually gets what he needs when he needs it) so I could feel like I was "doing my part," showing my love and appreciation for him!

Ouch! I didn't like admitting I was in ego. But then a childhood memory came forward. In it my mom was opening up a Christmas present from my dad. The backstory is that he had asked her what she wanted for Christmas and then drove her to the store in a snowstorm to get it. He then left it on the table with all the other presents for her to wrap!

On Christmas morning, she graciously opened it in front of everyone, smiled sweetly at my dad, and said, "Wouldn't it be funny if there were a $100 bill in this purse?" She opened it up, and there *was* a $100 bill there! My dad tried so hard to surprise her—making her buy it and wrap it! He had to go to a lot of trouble to find it, unwrap it carefully and rewrap it, so he could add that surprise. And then I knew the real reason I wanted to surprise my husband, and that is because I learned that surprises are a way we show our love and appreciation! Sometimes, being okay with what happens is the greater gift!

Take an Evolutionary Step Upward

Humanity is now being constantly bombarded with wonderful support-ive vibrations that are changing reality in such a way that it is easier and easier for you to be your fifth dimension self. Your daily prayer work and meditations, especially in groups, will help anchor it into reality. Even though everything is based on free will, your intention to open to receive abundance, healing, transformation, and mastery connect you with these vibrations and support your every decision. Imagine millions of dollars being dropped from a high-rise building. The people below still need to pick up the money and put it to use for themselves and humanity.

Some of this energy will help you move through the lower vibration of the ego. You have many opportunities to work with the ego. Seek out and learn the tools of connecting with the Higher Self (see chapter 1), which will also help you teach the ego—the benefit of the Higher Self connection. At some point you may be able to merge the ego with the Higher Self.

FIFTH-DIMENSIONAL BALANCING OF MALE AND FEMALE

When one of my sons was prepubescent, and I was teaching him that everyone comprises both male and female, he emphatically told me, "Mom, there is nothing female inside of me!" I smiled at his outburst. Ideally both men and women aspire to develop the balanced self, which is the full expression of the divine feminine and divine masculine in either sex. It is conveyed through the physical expressions of compassion and receptivity on the female side, and the expressions of balance, order, and power on the masculine side. Each of us is called to this balance and will continue to encounter all of these aspects until we have achieved mastery through this balance.

In 5D your expression can be either inwardly or outwardly depending on the situation and needs of the moment. (Think of men who take care of their children and women who are operating machinery.) This gives you tremendous flexibility. Imagine being able to switch to a masculine or feminine way of being—depending on the person or situation you are in. Women and men have been doing this, almost spontaneously, for quite some time.

Having stayed at home with my children for a few years after being in the corporate world, I didn't realize I'd turned into an "Earth Mother." Yet when I went back to work, I adopted my former corporate ways. Then I was coming back home at night still wearing my "corporate, masculine hat." I discovered I was creating havoc at home with my family by bringing home my masculine ways. Once I realized this, I consciously "changed hats" from corporate (male)-type energy to nurturing (female), and the home chaos evaporated. This new balance is the 5D way. As you connect and immerse yourself in your true identity, you may discover it is very easy to express either male or female expressions or both male and female polarities almost simultaneously.

The Divine Male and Divine Female Healed

Since early 2006 we have been dealing with the gestation and birth of the divine male and divine female in the human. We are now moving through the infancy and "learning to talk" stage. The next phases can be compared to toddler, adolescent, and, finally, adulthood. Your goal is to reinvent yourself and evolve into the new vibrations.

The divine male grid, an energetic basis for how males act, react, and resolve leadership behaviors, has been upgraded. Originally the divine male was a follower of the alpha male and the energy of the divine female was that of support. In the new 5D version, each male may lead himself and will be able to work together with other males in a more egalitarian way. This is best explained by examining the old way of leadership.

In the days of the Knights Templar, male action was much different. A Grail Knight followed the mission of a Servant of the Grail. It was his job to protect and serve the leader of the group. A man's partner in the Grail work was concealed and unknown. His family was not in the picture, although these men often had families. The hidden families were called the Friends of the Grail. These Friends of the Grail lived in communities where their true identity would never be discovered, to protect the woman and the children of these unions. This matrix, with the woman following, being low profile, and supportive, was a part of an earlier mission of contracts between men and women.

There has been a bigger mission running in the background for many individuals working with Mary Magdalene. On our first Mary Magdalene Sacred Journey in 2006 something shifted when we came together in France. On the last day of our trip we were in a very sacred place, near Ussat, France, with a member of the bloodline of Mary Magdalene. It was she who anointed us and conducted a ceremony where the men stood in for the men of humanity and women stood in for the women of humanity. In that ceremony, men advanced from the position of Servants of the Grail to Champions of the Grail. Women advanced from being Friends of the Grail to Companions of the Grail. These new matrices empowered men and women to be their divine selves, no longer locked into positions based on loyalty to a person.

Men being activated to champions meant they didn't have to prove anything or conquer anything to establish their worth. They also didn't need to follow a leader. Importantly, they no longer were required to abandon their family to accomplish their mission! As champions they could pick and choose their work expression, which might include working with others. The women were activated as companions, true equals, partnering in every way (*companion* in Old English means "spouse") as equals. This means the grids of Servants and Friends were replaced with the new energy of Champion and Companions.

However, more work was needed for this to be integrated into reality. This took longer than expected. In the meantime, men and women everywhere were finding their way within these new grids, announcing their clear intention to be different from their predecessors.

In 2012 Mayan shaman Hunbatz Men led a sacred journey with me and other spiritual teachers. At our ceremonies he reminded all of us this is the age of the woman, that men will need to step aside. Many spiritual teachers are saying this. At this event, I "accepted" this mantle of spiritual leader on behalf of all women and reminded our audience that it is incumbent upon all of us, especially women, that this is a new power of equality and shared leadership.

The 2014 Magdalene Sacred Journey was an extension of the grace of our earlier journey. The champion (male) was given healing from the wound of manipulation and overwhelm. The companion (female) was given healing from overpowering and subjugation! Anchoring in the antidote of these wounds was just part of the ceremony. We also claimed the *consolamentum* for each member of our group on behalf of humanity. This "sacrament of the Cathars" was the equivalent of the immersion in the Holy Spirit—or Divine Union. Consolamentum was a ceremony done exclusively in the cave where we were; in the ceremony a candidate became a "perfect"—fully plugged into his or her God self. We activated ourselves, asking our Higher Selves to do the anointing. The healing of these wounds created a connection of equal power and harmony between the genders.

Many similar ceremonies are occurring all over the planet to heal and unify old emotional wounds created by excesses that caused abuses. Allowing for and creating ceremonies and rituals is one key to accomplishing much in the new energies. This is an important way for you to bring in a level of mastery and connection between you and your Divine Self. Connect with your heart, and work with them.

9
Recognizing the Higher Dimensions

So far, we have been discussing the first five dimensions, but there are actually thirteen dimensions, all of which can be accessed. I have provided a quick reference table at the end of this section to initiate your exploration of the dimensions, including their values and their characteristics. You truly are multidimensional, and these landmarks will help you identify your location in any given moment. Ultimately they will help you comprehend that you are simultaneously oscillating between multiple dimensions while mostly focusing on one at a time.

One of the features of 5D is that you become more aware of reality's aberrations. If you saw the movie *The Matrix,* this would compare to the scene when Neo (the protagonist) sees a cat move forward, backward, and then forward again. He mentions this, and his escorts into the matrix recognize it as the cue to get out of the matrix immediately. This film is definitely worth seeing if you truly want to understand the dimensions, as much of the principles are readily transferable. Because there is violence, I also recommend you cover your chakras while watching it.*

Becoming aware of reality's anomalies occurs because you can

---

*A simple hand movement placing your palm above the top of your head about six inches, and then moving your hand down the front of your body, keeping the distance, and intending each of the chakras is closed, like manually closing one's eyes. The chakras will easily reopen on their own later.

readily discern manufactured lies from the news media and disinformation counterintelligence when you are no longer plugged into the mass consciousness mind control being aimed at humanity. You can no longer be lied to without "noticing" that something "isn't right." Much of what was once the cloud of disinformation suddenly becomes patently clear. How do you step into this awareness? One way is to begin to understand what each of the upper dimensions has to offer—and how you can experience them. In later chapters we will discuss methods to step out of the lockdown in third dimension.

Tables 9.1, 9.2, and 9.3 on pages 173 through 175 outline the primary characteristics of the thirteen dimensions, divided into three realms: lower or polarity creation, middle creation, and upper creation. The benefit of being able to identify the various dimensions allows you to consciously move to those locations in your meditations, and then eventually you'll intuitively add them into your conscious, waking environment. This skill also helps you understand that at every level, there is order, congruency, and focus.

The basic evolutionary steps that we are moving through give us insight as to what's next. The lower creation should help you understand what you already know and experience. Through this understanding, you can begin contemplation of the higher dimensions.

From my perspective, this information is helpful to the linear mind, which is always seeking to understand. You can let your spiritual work lead and eventually become fifth dimensional, or you can choose to use both your mind and your spiritual work. This means adopting a mental attitude to recognize and observe in yourself—either through self-introspection, your close friends, or your behaviors—beliefs or attitudes that are conflicting with the fifth-dimensional concept. This allows you to anchor yourself at a higher place than you would have been able to do if you just did your heart work. We often feel safer with our spouse or close family and friends where we exhibit our worst behavior. This is the ideal setting to change if we will allow it. In the end, it is simply a system of information that assists your understanding so you can get out of your own way. Just as you learn to suspend disbelief while at the movies, allowing yourself to coexist in more than one reality, now is the time to let your ego mind allow your multidimensional possibilities! As you become more accepting of this and aware of each dimension's unique qualities, you can access them intentionally.

Humans are already occupying multiple dimensions simultaneously. There are multiple versions of you that are currently participating in other dimensions. This fact is counterintuitive because one of the functions of 3D is an assemblage point, so the observer and the experiencer are one person, eliminating the awareness of other expressions. This is one of the things that is now changing. In fact your experiences in creation are also replicating the *relationships* between the dimensions, as well as their specific qualities. In addition, understanding and accepting this concept of the dimensions provides a unique way of layering the information of an individual's experiences in the reality. It helps you to recognize that while you may be fifth dimensional in any moment, the dimensions are vibrationally nested, like Russian dolls. This means you may still interact with your family, who may be third dimensional only because at any level you have access to experience lower levels. There are rules about the form that interaction takes, but that mostly applies to fifth dimension and above. Study the chart at the end of this section to help you identify the qualities of each of the dimensions. Armed with this new understanding you can begin to see that the relationships between creations are as important as the actual creations themselves.

The symmetry and order found in the physical world and in the universe, in all forms of sacred geometry such as music, visual aids, or wearable art, assist mankind in reweaving or calibrating their old, dysfunctional patterns and irregularities into their own divine blueprint. There are many new artists working in this medium.

Working through the tables on pages 173 through 175, you can see some basic structure around the dimensions. We have already discussed the dimensions up to the fifth, but below we look into those beyond the fifth dimension as well.*

Sixth dimension is the place where we often go to during the dreamtime. It is a place that has structure and form if we desire it—but doesn't require it. It is the place of all templates for basic structures on Earth, such as DNA, geometry, and light languages, that form the basis for developed expressions and experiences in third dimension. In sixth dimension, you are so sated with individuality from the fifth you are ready to begin to express in groups. Yet the structure of group is still being refined. This is the zone where you might begin to recognize other versions of you and recognize your work in someone else.

Seventh dimension is coming in directly from Source, yet it carries the material aspect of precision. The basis for group expression is found here. As such, this is the last place one can experience oneself as separate. Seventh dimension is a place where you feel such sweet emotional connection with consciousness, as expressed through souls similar to you, that manifestation in groups comes easily.

Eighth dimension is so vast that from our vantage point in third dimension it is difficult to comprehend. In the eighth dimension one cannot experience the self as separate. Generally, when consciousness is focused here, the third-dimensional self blanks out; the force of life becomes the collective, collaborative whole. Although groups exist in this domain, the limitlessness of consciousness permeates. This is the arena where you are more *we* than *me*.

Ninth dimension represents the collective consciousness of dissimilar groups: planets, star systems, galaxies, and dimensions; yet awareness is inner directed. This specific inner direction creating collective consciousness works just as the dissimilar parts of the human body as a whole make up a great system.

Tenth dimension is where the beings of the basis for creation exist. Their energy is so vast it is really beyond our initial ability to understand. This is where the divine blueprint is formed. This is the source of the

---

*More on all of the dimensions can be found in my book *Beyond the Flower of Life*.

Elohim and other divine beings and systems. It is Source code at its finest.

Eleventh dimension is a wonderful place of anticipation. It is the place where concept is more alive than form. It is an environment of the integrated awareness of the separated parts of God, held in a place of union and communion. The place of union is so ecstatic that it defies description. We find the Akashic Records are here. Remember, the Akashic Records are a living field that shifts and changes. Even though we use the word "records," which implies permanence, it is more of a living, breathing environment. Eleventh is the region of the Archangels, Lord Metatron, and mathematical codes, which include the genetic codes for the expression of all the versions of the reality. It also contains a quality of euphoria that would be akin to the moment before orgasm. Once you have experienced this dimension, you really are never the same being as before.

The twelfth dimension is the place of Pure Consciousness and Light Consciousness. It is the environment that is so connected to itself that there is no separation of any kind. It is, for some, the stopping point of creation.

The thirteenth dimension appears to me as Unity Consciousness and a place for new beginnings. I have experienced this energy as the place where any thoughts of not-God would cause pain and are truly unthinkable. Love is the essence of all here, and even this descriptive is insufficient.

One of the ways to experience multidimensionality is to completely blank out. Generally, when you forget what you saw or did in your meditation, you've gone so high that there is no reference point. Another way the mind deals with the overload of changing the way you experience and understand the world around you is forgetfulness. You are about to do something, and then you realize that you've forgotten what you were thinking about and you are afraid it might be serious. This forgetfulness is an ideal moment for consciousness to completely disengage from one version of the reality to another.

Each of these moments is a form of unhooking from the ego's holding-on mechanisms. If it has been happening a lot lately, consider the fact that you may be jumping dimensions and that you simply aren't able to hold your awareness in both yet.

Over the years, so much information has come through the teaching of this material, yet I still find that the largest capacity to comprehend will come from use of the tables below to help you summarize and experience each dimension. You can also find additional information in my book *Beyond the Flower of Life.*

TABLE 9.1.
FIRST THROUGH FOURTH DIMENSION:
LOWER OR POLARITY CREATION REALM

Dimension	States of Being	What We Find Here
1st	Inner focused, self-awareness, will of God	point of self-awareness
2nd	Outer focused, point and line, single surface (like a piece of paper), wisdom of God	Recognizing relationship oriented toward self and other, beginning of polarity
3rd	Inner focused, matter based, active intelligence, devotion to God; place where we integrate individuality with godliness, learn to hurt and heal; sound and color from higher dimensions emanates from one's body and (toning) reweaves it into a functional pattern, ceremony—words, ceremony—actions *Goal: balancing* experiences of polarity by integrating matter and contrast; *matter based*	Creating Heaven on Earth, projection from other dimensions, drama of good and evil, polarity consciousness; appearance of number *and* relationship, such as irrational "constants" as *pi* and *phi* become the basis for creation in matter; ever-present polarity consciousness caused by loneliness for God causes occasional desire to escape 3D into heaven! *Goal:* work toward balance and use desire to create Heaven on Earth!
4th	Outward focused, elemental kingdom mostly from 4D; purity of God (art, music culture); projecting elemental kingdom (gnomes, fairies, elves, magic) *Goal:* learn to balance the world of spirit, *emotionally based*	Extremely mutable dimension. High: movement upward (to 5D), low: astral plane—place of seduction, easy to get caught/stuck here, polarity forces still operating

TABLE 9.2.
FIFTH THROUGH NINTH DIMENSION:
MIDDLE CREATION REALM

Dimension	States of Being	What We Find Here
5th	Inner focused, Christ consciousness, light bodies; evidence of God (science) *Goal:* balance all aspects of the self as expressed through the Higher Self, ultimate of human perfection, *spiritually based*	Heaven by the 3D standards; perfection as we know it; bliss, projection of conceived perfection, fully integrated, aware of greater states of being, involving group consciousness
6th	Outward focused, peace and idealism, all symbolic language is used here; individual bodies still exist but live much longer than in 3D; use of the MerKaBa and other sacred geometry to support creative endeavors and unify purposes; control of physical matter of one's body, molding it to thoughts, moving in groups, *group form based*	Realm of color, light, music, geometry, DNA templates (patterns of all types of species), co-creation with others, creating form, working during sleep; consciousness creates from thought, has a body only if it desires
7th	Inner focused, manifestation from source, lucid light, clear tone, clear geometry and pure expression, like a school of fish—separate yet moving "as one," *group expression based*	Place of infinite precision, perceive self as the "individual"
8th	Outward focused, group mind, group soul, more "we" than "me," awareness centered on the group as "us" (school of fish group movement), collective = one heart, one mind, one being, *group consciousness based*	Vast proportions beyond 3D comprehension, difficult to keep consciousness together if traveling from 3D (one might go to sleep or black out at this dimension; the body elemental "shuts down" all activities here and beyond)

9th	Inner focused, collective consciousness of planets, star systems, galaxies, and dimensions; group consciousness of dissimilar groups, *collective consciousness based,* vastness	Inner awareness greater than outer awareness (one is part of complex whole), everything more vast than our understanding of consciousness

TABLE 9.3.
TENTH THROUGH THIRTEENTH DIMENSION:
UPPER CREATION REALM

Dimension	States of Being	What We Find Here
10th	Outward focused, new plans developed, the beings of the base of creation; *creation in matter based*	Appearance of divine blueprint, building blocks, sense of individuality (not to the degree of 5D)
11th	Inner focused, process rather than beingness, a place of anticipation, preformed light, Metatron, archangels, Akashic Records for planet, galaxy, and entire system; the Akashic Records are alive!; *pregnant (expectancy) based*	Environment of beloved union (love of separate parts of God too ecstatic for description); point before creation/a state of exquisite expectancy (knowing imminence of creation cannot be resisted), union to potentiality, ecstasy before conception
12th	Outward focused, one awareness of all, one force, one God, one light, no separation (redundant), the ability to experience one God; *light consciousness based*	Return to one point, all consciousness knows itself to be utterly One with All That Is, no separation of any kind, forever touched/altered by knowing who you really are
13th	Inner focused, *unity consciousness based*	Love is the essence of *all*!; compassionate readiness

HOW ARE THEY BASED?

Each category has a basis of operation. This means that the overlay that occurs in each dimension is ruled by this expression. Third dimension is matter based, fourth dimension is emotionally based, fifth dimension is spiritually based, sixth dimension is group form based, seventh dimension is group expression based, eighth dimension is group consciousness based, and so on.

A way to begin understanding this is to recognize that we are all already operating within these structures without realizing it. For example, the woman who started Mothers Against Drunk Driving (MADD) went through a matter experience—her daughter died. Then she dealt with her emotions of grief that created the emotional basis. Then she went into service through spiritualizing the experience by finding a purpose to help others because of her loss.

She then formed a group, the group developed its own expressions—including speaking before Congress. Then MADD became a symbol or consciousness based in their developed partnerships (for example, with American Automobile Association, or AAA) and the group's own culture. In the final stages, MADD had created countless additional partnerships and a collective consciousness that is widely known and accepted.

As you move into the Higher Creation realm of tenth through thirteenth dimension, the analogy goes further into the esoteric, but it helps you to realize that you are very likely pursuing advancement on multiple dimensions at the same time. You can start to identify this as you look at your own life and what interests you along with how you are expressing through those interests.

Most people are on the even-numbered dimensions or the odd-numbered dimensions. Even-numbered dimensions are introspective and internally oriented while odd-numbered dimensions tend to be outward based or expansive. Another way to look at it is to say that any odd-numbered dimension has an action quality to it or is male compared to the even-numbered dimensions that tend to be introspective and receptive or female. All of this is very exciting as you start to realize how very similar the macrocosm and the microcosm are to each other.

An Experience of Going Beyond Eighth Dimension

One of my friends and hosts from Bulgaria wrote me a moving e-mail that confirms some of this information about experiencing the higher dimensions.

"Today was the first day of a very advanced workshop called Mahatma Initiations. We were doing a work in what you call 7, 8, and 9 dimensions, and the love was immense. We were clearing old creations, patterns, and intensions, realities for us that no longer serve us, and so on. At the end we created a program for abundance, prosperity, love, and light, and the sensation was a pure bliss. After that I left the people to create their own programs.

"One woman lost consciousness at the end of the meditation. She was just sitting on the chair—no breathing, no pulse—her body tried to assume the fetus position in the womb of a mother. We 'awaked her' (so no problem) but she told us that she intended to return herself to the source and she was experiencing only pure golden light and deep love and nothing else—no thoughts. She said she was everywhere in creation and it lasted hours. I am saying this to you only as confirmation to when you said that the body elemental is switching off the body if your mind wanders beyond the 8th dimension. Don't worry—it wasn't scary. The people were so calm and we were speaking only in love after that event."

DIMENSIONAL SHIFTS

In order to help you understand the dimensions, what follows are a few examples of what it might be like to be aware of more than one dimension. This can happen in a variety of ways. You may be able to perceive colors and sounds and scents that were not available to you prior to this time. Or you may have feelings of "spacy-ness" that seem off the chart! Once upon a time—when I accidentally got MSG poisoning—I felt myself leave my body and felt quite "disconnected" from reality. It can be a bit like that. Even if you are sitting down, if you feel like you still have to stabilize yourself, it may very well be that you are experiencing dimensional shifts!

Hearing the Tone

Some people hear a loud tone immediately following that feeling. Rest assured that this too is part of your new normal. What's really going on is that it is as if you are lifting a heavy table up the stairs and stopping to catch your balance. Imagine that a few strong souls who can shift and change—and do—are carrying a heavy table up the stairs a few steps at a time, allowing pauses to rest, and then they shift and change again. The loud tone that is coming in is the "anchoring" signal that all of the shifting is happening and it's okay and to keep going.

Seeing the Light

Some of the individuals in my inner circle are also seeing lights. In one particular experience, a woman who has blackout shades placed on her windows woke up in the middle of the night and could see bright balls of light. Initially she was scared, but she was able to cognitively decide that her vision was *not* of anything in her room and to check in with me. I too had been seeing them. You may be as well, and the reason for it may surprise you.

It means you are registering or seeing as your 5D self while also being in 3D. Welcome to the fifth dimension! Seeing the lights in the corner of your eye midday is also a common experience. (This is not the same as dark spots known as floaters, which come as people age!) When you notice these beings, who, by the way, have been around for a while, give them a nod, smile, and welcome, saying, "If you are of the light, I invite you into my space to be of service to me and those around me!" Doing this turns on your wisdom channel in the moment.

10
Becoming Fifth Dimensional and Activating the Higher Chakras

Your chakras are wheels, gateways, and energy centers that have multiple purposes. They are receptors and transmitters. An immense body of literature has been written about the seven-chakra system, and it is a worthwhile study. My intent here is to help you learn about, open to, and activate your higher chakras (8–12). Activating these higher chakras opens you up to the realm of spiritual gifts formerly reserved for the Buddhas. In fact Buddha means "awakened one."

All the chakras are open and available to anyone. We will begin with a brief look at each of the higher chakras to learn what they do and how you can connect with them. Like the dimensions, the chakras alternate being inwardly focused and outwardly focused. In the 3D expression of being, the chakras primarily express in an inward or outward way. In men the root, solar plexus, throat, and crown are masculine or outwardly expressed. For women the root, solar plexus, throat, and crown chakras are expressing in an inwardly way.

The chakras do not necessarily open in sequential order but stimulate each other for gradual awakening at all levels. It is also true that as one chakra opens, the one beneath it is energized and subsidized, so the learning curve is very fast. Some of you have already opened and activated your upper chakras without any external effort or awareness. Some of you who are Ascended Masters are gently releasing the energies of these higher chakras as you learn to operate at the higher frequencies. You already have full access but usually choose to elevate yourself slowly, so as to not cause problems for yourself or others.

PINEAL GLAND ACTIVATION

Before we get into the higher chakras, it is important to briefly discuss the pineal gland and the third eye chakra. Twentieth century psychic and medical clairvoyant Edgar Cayce said, "Keep the pineal gland operating and you won't grow old . . . you will always be young."*

If you are serious about the activations and the energies moving through you, you will do well to make a few choices to improve your results. The following list of suggestions is simply to help you understand that old programmer's phrase, "garbage in—garbage out." Give yourself these gifts as best you can. Any shift in this direction will help you.

1. Avoid fluoridated water. This calcifies the pineal gland, thus halting its activity.
2. Avoid wheat, gluten, and sugar. These slow down the high vibrational expressions, and in some cases completely limit them.
3. Clear heavy metals, mercury, aluminum, and other toxins out of your water, and detox your body of these metals. There is much recourse for metals detox.
4. Meditate daily. Build your practice so you are hungry for meditation when you skip it.
5. Eat organic and as much raw food as you can.
6. Exercise daily.

---

*This quote comes from a reading given for Edgar Cayce himself in which information was sought on Cayce's psychic process. Since many previous readings had mentioned the importance of the pineal gland in connection with psychic experiences, this was certainly a reasonable request.

7. Get sun exposure. Check out alternative health expert Dr. Joseph Mercola's website[1] to learn more about vitamin D and sun exposure. See also the TED talk on the same subject (sun exposure) by dermatologist and researcher Dr. Richard Weller.[2]

8. Sleep regularly. Many have overlooked the very important detail about sleep. They see it as a necessary evil. Yet sports teams to businessmen are learning that sleep improves performance at all levels of existence.[3]

Each of these items is the subject of much readily available information. These basic suggestions will make it easier for you to achieve and maintain your fifth-dimensional state. As you explore these new commitments to yourself, you will begin to identify and notice that your subconscious mind gives you clues.

Connecting to God

There may be some moments that you are seriously questioning what is going on! Each of us has the ability to connect directly to God through our opening in the third eye and our central column, the pranic tube. Some experience the rapid opening of the river of energy that leads to the pineal gland as an "event." In older Eastern traditions, these events, sometimes termed "kundalini awakenings," were limited to spiritual teachers and leaders. Today this can happen to anyone—and it may in fact be your wake-up call to the spiritual work you are intending to do.

Initially, this can be frightening if you don't know what is happening. As this process occurs, you may experience this river of energy flowing in your pranic tube as greatly increased. One of the most magical opportunities is to begin recognizing that you are broadcasting your energy daily. Knowing this, you can consciously choose to stay centered and in your heart.

Deepening your awareness of the energy that moves through you is very powerful. Most of us think that we are receiving information through the mind. What I know now is that our mind is simply grabbing the information that comes through the heart and then solving and sorting it for us.

Allow yourself to discover this by paying attention to changes in the energy around your heart. Many individuals are actively storing information in this area. One of the ways to open yourself to this work is through the work of Tom Kenyon. You might start with his wonderful guided meditation called White Gold Alchemy.[4] This will teach you to activate the channels from your heart to your pineal gland. This opens the way for your Higher Self connection.

Activate the Dodecahedron around the Heart

There is a dodecahedron around the heart that serves as the receptor of information from higher dimensions. This serves as a portal for divine communication from other dimensions. When the mind is quiet—either while doing mundane peaceful activities, such as hiking in nature, doing dishes, or meditation—we are able to open the channel of communication. We can open the heart many ways; one way is to bring in the Higher Self, but sometimes this happens in other ways, such as a blow to the heart.

A blow to the heart is an opportunity to be hurt by someone you know and love and whom you expect to do much better. You aren't expecting the letdown, which is why it is so effective in getting you to change, to shift, to let go, to open up. All of these or one of these actions is the net result of the blow to the heart. Finally, the last stage of the blow to the heart is to keep your heart open!

Disinformation Abounds

There are many, many disinformation agents in the emerging spirituality and the fields of health, commerce, and more. Look into homeopathy on Wikipedia, then check out Bing's definition. Actually, you will find this disinformation in all arenas—and no doubt you've uncovered a few yourself. Consider this—without the ability to discern, how will you know if a cure, treatment, or therapy is right? How will you know what to do in your own circumstance, your family's, and more? You must use your Higher Self!

It is helpful to work in groups, which will help you to discover that some information is found to be inappropriate for anyone, because everyone in the group gets similar information from their guidance. Continue to be suspicious of anything that doesn't feel right, or anything that your study group in general has doubts about.

Sometimes individuals spreading the disinformation may not even know they are agents of it. Discerning disinformation is paramount to being fifth dimensional. The good news is that once you are fifth dimensional—once you become 5D—disinformation becomes obvious for what it is.

ACCESSING THE HIGHER CHAKRAS

Waking up in 5D grants you access to the higher chakras. Here are some indications of what you can expect as they open and energize. You can begin to recognize when your higher chakras are open or are opening by virtue of the energy qualities moving through them as they become available to you. They serve to provide humans with information they cannot receive through their five senses. Using these higher chakras signals the universe you are ready to begin a higher dimensional frequency life.

The Eighth Chakra

This is the chakra above the head. As you open your eighth chakra, you might feel a tingling or pressure above your head. Its purpose is to connect you to your evolved self as a 5D human. It is the birth canal of the upper gateway and as such gives birth to the activation of the five secret chakras and the five secret rays. The five secret chakras are located in the palms of your hands, soles of your feet, and near the spleen or thymus.

When you use your hands to do any form of energy work, they turn back negative energy. The feet allow anchoring into the zero chakra (discussed on page 187) and connect you to the energies of the Earth. These secret rays are anchored through the right brain. The secret chakra of the spleen also channels through breastfeeding. Hidden within them are powers to heal and help humanity and the Earth. The five secret rays are contained within the white and yellow rays of the rainbow. They are activated naturally as you open to your eighth chakra.

The eighth chakra, known as the secret chamber of the heart, opens you to a level of unconditional love so great that you carry a compassion for all life, which is known as divine love. This divine love can now flow through you. It represents your connection to all of life. As you grow your compassion and concern for others, situations, and circumstances, your eighth chakra becomes activated and vice versa! This means as you do meditation and activations that open this chakra, it then becomes easier and easier to have and hold compassion for your fellow human beings.

This energetic portal raises your awareness to more than who you are as a physical being. It creates an inner peace, as well as an inner connection with others. This inner connection is already known in the animal kingdom. The Greek naturalist Pliny the Elder defined it in dolphins, but it can now also be ascribed to humans: *friendship for no advantage.*

Everywhere you go, you are discovering that sweet friendship between strangers that barely existed before. Some say this is where karma resides, but for all practical purposes karma doesn't exist any more because of the dispensations that are available to humanity (see chapter 4). I encourage you to claim your new inheritance; there is no more karma!

People are experiencing the eighth chakra in many ways. The color I experience is iridescent purple/green with gold. Its new location is above the head, yet it is often felt between the heart and throat chakra on certain individuals.

Ninth Chakra

As you open and activate this chakra, you begin to be aware of your true cosmic blueprint. In some traditions, this is the energy of the causal body, the "storehouse in heaven." This is most often depicted as a spherical rainbow around a center body, the causal body. This chakra will help you heal your wounds and allows you to begin controlling your reality. It connects you with the sun and solar system. It is a multidimensional portal. With this chakra open, you can bring in abundance, awareness, and connection to your time-space continuum. Through your ninth chakra opening you can witness multiple versions of yourself. As this cosmic temple becomes more available to you, your cosmic connections increase and your inner wisdom and outer wisdom move into sync.

Tenth Chakra

The tenth chakra is your earned mastery from previous embodiments or lifetimes. This chakra resonates with the great central sun system of our Milky Way galaxy. As this chakra opens, you gain access to certain mastery from other lifetimes, certain gifts that are not readily available to humans. You are able to accurately gather information, connect your own wisdom channel, and hear your angels' and guides' wisdom clearly. This is the active energy reflecting the mastery of past lives.

This chakra opens up at a very early age, sometimes even before adulthood, in those souls who are already Ascended Masters. They become self-aware that they can do things others cannot do. Because of their mastery, they usually remain humble. They often set up life experiences as children to insure they will not be operating from a place of ego. For instance, they may have an unusually demanding parent or sibling that tries to "hold them back." Since they know only love, this doesn't really matter, other than serving to condition them to be helpful and understanding to others, and to keep their humility. Contrarily, one who has had a difficult childhood and faces narcissistic tendencies is one who is in survival mode; such a one cannot see only love, unlike those who have achieved mastery and are back in embodiment to assist with the transformation of humanity.

Eleventh Chakra

The eleventh chakra portal is usually accessed through your devotion to the Divine. In physical terms it resonates with our entire galaxy as a living entity. All understanding is yours; you no longer need polarity to operate in your life. Decisions, all of them, flow through with grace and ease. There is a tendency, with this chakra open, to move into complacency, because the loving of the Divine is peaceful and heartfelt.

To stay motivated while this chakra is open and activated, keep your awareness on your Earth Star chakra (described on page 187). In this way you can complete your projects and your missions. This might be perceived as your magic carpet, because this chakra's opening will gift you with the abilities to time travel, bilocate, read energy of others, and precipitate material things. Perhaps you've heard of yogis who precipitate *vibhuti* (a white powdery substance) or jewels. However, instantaneous precipitation could be of anything material. This comes when you have the mastery to manage it.

Twelfth Chakra

This opening allows you to be completely connected to your Divine Self. Some have actually created a direct channel to God. Nikola Tesla was one such initiate. The twelfth chakra will help you complete your God mastery. While in embodiment, these skills are not always noticeable as different because when you are in this state of activation, you don't notice what is different (mostly because you have moved out of judgment and attachments).

THE ZERO CHAKRA

The zero chakra is just below the feet. It is often called the Earth Star chakra. Its purpose is to give you a deep connection to Mother Earth so you experience your own welfare and the Earth's as one. As a new chakra, it has no debris from other ages to hold you back from your sincere connection to the New Earth.

It also enables you to be a part of the new vision for the Earth, a very important function you can hold just by being connected to it! As you expand your upper connections, it is important that you stay connected to Mother Earth at the same time. This means that you are to remain in a body, while expanding your awareness through meditations. This is new, and this is unique to your 5D expression. Formerly these "high vibrational states" were only available to you if you shut down your body in a stillness-type meditation. Certainly you will use your stillness meditations to activate and line up all the energy centers (chakras) using this alignment to connect and heal. Now you will also gradually be able to maintain this state in your waking, walking state! You will be able to harbor both your divine and earthly connection simultaneously!

This connection to your Earth Star, especially after you activate your upper chakras, will anchor you in your body while simultaneously allowing you to be connected to your Divine Self. This chakra connects you to the whole planet. This new heart center allows you access to what's really going on—on planet Earth! As you open this portal, you can assist with the healing of planet Earth. The chakra has been put in place to serve you when staying in a body, while simultaneously holding an enlightened state. You can also help calm the Earth, and step into resolving Earth disruptions in the Earth's crust and in the Earth's weather by your clear intent.

MEDITATION

Meditation is crucial to bridging the gap between what the heart perceives and the mind receives! Even Edgar Cayce taught about meditation. In the Cayce readings (281–41), he says about meditation that:

It is not musing, not daydreaming; but as ye find your bodies made up of the physical, mental and spiritual, it is the attuning of the mental body and the physical body to its spiritual source.

Mindfulness meditation is very popular now. It is the emptying of the mind to make room for nothingness. Mindfulness is extremely useful, as it prepares you to receive the unlimited recourses of the universe. If your mind is always busy sorting, analyzing, examining, it doesn't have room for spontaneous knowledge. All the great thinkers know this. Many of the world's greatest discoveries occurred in the dream or meditative state. Mindfulness meditation plays an important role in helping you be open to new and undiscovered ideas, creativity, and more. It is a meditation form where the total goal is to have complete mental stillness.

Mindfulness has been well studied, and science has consistently proven it produces amazing beneficial results.[5] Mind the mind that minds! Your mind can hold you hostage to its interpretation of your experiences. *When you allow yourself to let go of the ego's stronghold on the messages of your mind, you will be open to receive the messages of the heart, and you will succeed in becoming fifth dimensional.* When you focus your attention on *now,* your self-awareness is unlimited. Humanity is being gifted by the presence of more and more refined energies to make your meditation easier and more meaningful.

Mindfulness is not the only kind of meditation. Specific guided meditation is also highly useful because it allows you to create energetic fields beyond what you can do without this practice. The MerKaBa meditation mentioned in chapter 2 is one such meditation. If you have the ability to do the MerKaBa meditation, I highly recommend it.* Now there is an even more evolved MerKaBa that allows you to take the activation to higher chakras, making it easier and easier to access and

---

*MerKaBa Classic is available on DVD so you can learn the original formula; see Suggested Resources.

utilize these energies. Once activated, your higher chakras are geared to run these energies efficiently. It will take you to a far more advanced place in your meditations.

This is not just an idle promise. The 5D MerKaBa connects you to an expanded energy field, grows your pranic tube, and then centers your energy field in such a way that you are reaching higher fields of consciousness as well as connecting to Mother Earth. This expansion aids Mother Earth in a way that allows you to tune into her, and she into you. It means you become part of the solution. It means you learn to "think like Mother Earth" in a way that serves both you and the Earth. It also helps you plug in and tune in to your most evolved self.

An Expanded MerKaBa Appears

In May of 2007 a being capable of connecting with all universes simultaneously came out of the great silence and channeled through, much like moving through a wormhole in space, the dimensions into this reality. This being introduced a new energetic frequency into this 3D plane of existence. It serves as the vehicle that will allow us to move to and hold the 5D frequencies that will move and sustain us as we move into our new world.

In that moment, the fifth dimensional MerKaBa was implanted into this plane of existence for humankind to be able to connect with and sustain those energies within the fifth dimension.

This being began first by anchoring the Rainbow Bridge, the traditional bridge between God and man, through the cosmic realm.* Using sacred geometry created for this purpose, it first intersected

---

*To think of a rainbow as the bridge to the Divine is common throughout world mythology. Raymond L. Lee Jr. and Alistair B. Fraser, authors of *The Rainbow Bridge: Rainbows in Art, Myth, and Science,* found the concept in Zulu, Navaho, Hawaiian, Japanese, Cambodian, Greek, Australian Aborigine, Chumash, and Hopi myths, as well as the Norse.

through the Pleiades and then through Arcturus.* From there it made a right angle, which created a pyramid. The energies of the Rainbow Bridge were anchored into three places (not revealed at this time) in the United States. Then new colors that the eighth and ninth Lords of Light—higher dimensional beings without individual names or identities—brought into this realm, crystalline teal and crystal-line magenta, were added. As the rainbow of energy was inserted through this grid's center crystal, it radiated out from this central crystal into all the crystals that were there, moving through all the crystal points and stretching into infinity. Many individuals are seeing these new colors—crystalline teal and crystalline magenta pink—in rainbows and various other visuals. All the 5D colors are transparent and crystalline.

This energy was stepped down through the Pleiades, which is the key needed to attune to this energy. *One who is attuned to and carries this energy may administer this activation.* In that moment, those 5D energies seeded the activation of the Fifth Dimensional MerKaBa, which is now implanted into this plane of existence for humankind to be able to connect with and be sustained in our journey of full Ascension into the fifth dimension.

------

*Arcturus of the constellation Boötes is the brightest star in the northern celestial hemisphere. With a visual magnitude of −0.05, it is the fourth brightest star in the night sky.

THE MOST POWERFUL MERKABA YET

The Multidimensional 5D MerKaBa is the most powerful MerKaBa on the planet. It will open you up to your fifth-dimensional self in a new and powerful way. An active third-dimensional MerKaBa is needed before one can sustain the Fifth-Dimensional MerKaBa. If you are *not* currently activating the 17-Breath MerKaBa and have never done it, please consider learning it before you take on this one. Follow your inner guidance on this.

The 5D MerKaBa meditation picks up with Activation Breaths 14–17. These energies build up from and rely on the building blocks of 3D geometric energies and expand them to even greater heights. It can be likened to a child's toy Transformer, which, with a few twists, turns, and stretches, becomes an advanced vehicle; similarly, this meditation offers greater power to propel travel much higher than could previously have been imagined.

With this new vehicle, one can now travel beyond the third and fourth dimensions, become grounded into the fifth dimension and even touch into the sixth. During this activation, an hourglass (a figure eight is a two-dimensional, flat, incomplete version) appears vertically. The lower loop will engulf your current third-dimensional existence. The crossing point will be the birth canal into the fourth dimension, which will then propel you forward into your new existence in the fifth dimension. You will then be able to touch into the sixth dimension. During this meditation, I literally experience it as a birth canal, seeing a vulva or a beautiful Georgia O'Keeffe lily painting.

The expanded energies produced from this more evolved and grounded MerKaBa will enable you to activate your eighth, ninth, tenth, eleventh, and twelfth chakras. It will pull in divine energy from beyond your current Higher Self connection and connect you with the cosmos. In addition, entering through this gate allows you to open up a portal that enables you to access energy tools from your eighth dimensional self.

Done correctly, with proper preparation, this new meditation almost always improves your other meditations and spiritual practices. It enhances your contentment and your flow of cosmic energy, as well as releasing the newer DNA frequencies to be reproduced in the body. Once you start to practice this new meditation, you may desire its continuation because it is so powerful at creating substantial changes by expanding who you really are! Indeed, many users find themselves reaching for this meditation about every forty-eight hours, as it is the vehicle to their new dawn and they "miss practicing it." I have personally observed close relationships with heart-centered humor and general goodwill and joy emanating from a person who is not typically a meditator but learned this meditation and started doing it regularly!

In addition, the serious students have been able to see the fine filaments coming from the causal body as one activates the 5D MerKaBa.) The causal body is your treasure house in heaven, meaning it is the repository of all your accomplishments from previous and current lifetimes. These filaments are mighty cosmos needle-like rays that reinforce the Earth. These rays are so fine that they cannot be measured, yet they are seen by some of the practitioners of this magnificent meditation.

The messenger of this material has chosen to remain anonymous, as her mission is to hold this for the Earth and humanity. She taught it to Janiece Jaffe, a beautiful soul, sound healer, and jazz singer who incubated it for a number of years before bringing it to me. Together we three women have brought it out to you. We agreed to have Janiece come to my Seattle home and offer training in sound healing and the Multidimensional MerKaBa. That training was sensational. We were all in awe of the experience of this meditation and the results we were achieving. You too will find the activation meditation and sound activation will open you to your higher chakras and your eighth dimensional and higher selves.

HOW DO I LEARN IT?

You can use the text and pictures provided on pages 194 to 200 to learn the meditation. We highly recommend that you also get the actual guided CD or the downloadable MP3 version (in a zip file to avoid losing sound that a normal compression software will create).* The recorded meditation consists of a fourteen-minute guided meditation with music by me

---

*Details on how to purchase the CD or downloadable file are given in Suggested Resources.

with illustrations by well-known Sacred Geometry artist, Endre Balogh[6] and a fifteen-minute voice activation by Janiece. This voice activation is so powerful that it releases the dark substance that resides in the four lower bodies—physical, mental, emotional, and etheric—which keeps us stuck in our current patterns, clears it, and then anchors in grids to hold the dimensional frequencies you have called in. The actual meditation is announced in detail for you, so you only need to visualize or imagine its action. We have also provided pictures to aid your visualization.

The energy you create from it is incredible. Almost everyone doing this activation is having significant experiences with it, including seeing certain vibrant colors, DNA images along with other images, and enjoyable body sensations. One particular body sensation is the clearing of the throat chakra and neck. While meditating with the CD many students have felt this "cleaning out" feeling of their neck being lengthened and straightened, as well as spine movements that seem to "click" the vertebra into alignment. More sensations such as improved eyesight, better health, and mental clarity have also been reported. One student says:

"I had some difficulties visualizing the 5D MerKaBa, so I focused in the feelings I had. I felt the vibration getting higher and higher, especially during the voice activation. Even though I didn't get completely clear about the instructions, I missed some words (English is my second language). Yet it definitely felt different. I was practicing over the last couple of weeks the original 17-Breath MerKaBa II meditation, and so I continued doing so before including the 5D MerKaBa. Very powerful indeed, it blew my mind, and left me speechless."

Below you will find the complete transcript of the guided meditation. What is missing is the sound activation that can only be achieved by listening to the recording.

MULTIDIMENSIONAL 5D MERKABA MEDITATION

This is the new 5D MerKaBa that was brought forward for your benefit, recorded by Maureen St. Germain with voice activation by

Janiece Jaffe. Ideally you are practicing the 17-Breath MerKaBa in preparation for activating this 5D MerKaBa. You will know if you need this step!

✳ MULTIDIMENSIONAL 5D MERKABA

This is a more advanced, highly evolved 5D MerKaBa. It will anchor your heart to your eighth chakra, activate higher dimensional energies, and help you keep your heart and mind open to your more advanced and evolved self.

The recording itself begins with the last three breaths of the original MerKaBa Classic. Remember to breathe unconditional love into your heart from both Earth and the cosmos.

1. Continue to hold your hands in the same mudra (as breath 14); see fig. 10.1: fingers nested, thumbs touching. Continue pranic breathing—deep meditative breathing where you visualize the prana entering the body from both the crown chakra and perineum simultaneously, flowing inward, never outward—throughout the rest of the meditation.

2. Now, see within your heart the flower of life as a sphere. It's actually multiple spheres: one spinning counterclockwise, one clockwise, and one spinning in both directions simultaneously. Now, as three spheres, they are a complete unit, spinning on the same axis as your pranic tube,

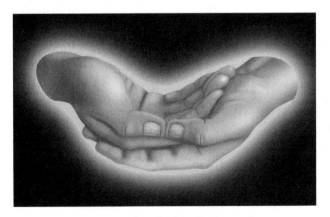

Figure 10.1. Mudra for MerKaBa meditation

emanating from your high heart chakra. It now changes colors to a teal-colored sphere with golden lines.

3. Next, let it expand slowly, enlarging while spinning to the size of your chest cavity. Take as much time as you need. Let it adjust for the perfect size for you. Focus your awareness on the following words: *Allow, Observe, Listen, Blissful-Unfolding.*

4. Invite your pranic flowing energy to support your flower of life sphere in slowly floating up your pranic tube—gently lifting and pulling with grace and ease, first moving up to the throat chakra, then the third eye, next to the crown chakra, and then continuing to go up—to the chakra above your head, centering the flower of life's spheres in your eighth chakra (see fig. 10.2).

*Figure 10.2. Center your flower of life sphere
in your eighth chakra above your head*

5. Your flower of life sphere is now centered completely in your eighth chakra above your head, in a location that is tied directly to your higher chakras. Allow.

6. At this point you will have created a figure-eight flow, with a new golden etheric body mirrored above your physical body. You may observe spirals throughout this field. You may also experience the upper and lower hourglass figures like the upper and lower parts of a clamshell (see fig. 10.3).

Figure 10.3. Figure-eight flow

7. You have created a beautiful figure eight in 2D and fully rounded hourglass in 3D. The figure-eight flow has a quality of moving around itself and within itself like a tube torus. It is built upon a figure eight spinning so rapidly upon itself that it appears as if it is pulsating dimensionally beyond what you are normally capable of seeing from your 3D perspective. Both the bottom and upper parts of the hourglass have this 5D way of moving (see fig. 10.4).

Figure 10.4. Figure-eight flow spinning upon itself

8. Keeping the center of your awareness and energy on your eighth chakra, your new heart center of unconditional love, you will *now* put your attention on the sun and earth tetrahedrons, located in the lower half of the hourglass shape.

9. Simultaneously move both points of the sun and earth tetrahedrons within themselves in opposite directions. The lowest point of the earth tetrahedron ascends from its place below the feet through the center of itself to the upper half of the hourglass, moving upward, along the pranic tube, beyond all the physical chakras, continuing upward past the crown chakra, upward past the eighth, ninth, tenth, eleventh, and twelfth chakras, locking into the top of the figure-eight hourglass. Your pranic tube has now extended to more than double its normal length, extending half its length above your head. As this occurs, notice that you gently activated your higher chakras as you crossed each threshold.

10. At the same time, the original sun tetrahedron's uppermost point moves downward, within itself along the pranic tube toward the earth, to the bottom of the hourglass, connecting into the zero chakra, and locking into Mother Earth. The zero chakra is a new chakra for most humans, and it assists you in keeping your connection to the Earth Star as you bring in these expanded connections.

11. Notice that anchoring your sphere of spinning flower of life energy on the eighth chakra opens you to a continuum and will slowly and gently assist you in the sweet opening of the higher chakras.

Your eighth chakra, your new heart center, is the center of divine love, spiritual compassion, and spiritual selflessness. Any unresolved karma has already been dissolved here, but you must choose to activate the spiritual skills that you have stored here.

As the ninth chakra begins to open, you are tapping into your soul's blueprint. This is the true storehouse of the outer skills showing up in the eighth chakra and gently feeding them.

In the tenth chakra, your creativity, synchronicities, and the merging of the divine masculine and the divine feminine are present. Allow yourself to activate this chakra, as you open to a new way of being centered, balanced, and powerful.

Your eleventh chakra allows you to access your inner ability of spiritual gifts that are beyond what is presently considered possible. This may include time travel, teleportation, or bilocation. You may also begin to experience the precipitation of virbuti or material objects. This is what we know the true bodhisattvas do. And you may accomplish this yourself. As this chakra starts to open, it has a monitoring effect, allowing it to become easier and easier for your lower chakras to benefit from this opening.

The twelfth chakra connects you perfectly to your *cosmic Divine Self,* which plugs you into all. Notice that anchoring your sphere of spinning flower of life energy on the eighth chakra opens you to this continuum and will slowly and gently assist you in the sweet opening of these higher chakras.

12. As you continue to bring in prana from both directions, the cosmos and the Earth, with your inhale, activate the lifting of the perineum up to the top of the new sun tetrahedron. The cosmic energy coming down through the pranic tube flows downward simultaneously. Your pranic flow is feeding your cosmic superhighway. And your pranic tube has now become home for your rainbow bridge, your personal connection to the Divine. The rainbow body is the actual form that appears when bodhisattvas spontaneously burst into light.

13. As you breathe, new crystalline structures and colors may appear. They may show up as vertical DNA spirals of beautiful shimmering, shifting, and fluctuating colors. The lower hourglass shape may appear heart chakra green, while the upper half of the hourglass shape may appear a bright purple, the color of the sixth chakra.

14. *Continue to breathe through this newly activated and extended pranic tube as long as you wish, insuring you are allowing prana to move in from both Earth and cosmos.* Continue to energize your flower of life sphere, nestled in the nexus of the rounded hourglass, centered on the eighth chakra above your head. As the hourglass interacts with itself, it creates

two tube toruses that are completely interacting with each other.

15. Allow this beautiful energy to build inside the flower of life shape. Remember, you may see one specific color or multiple colors, or a kaleidoscope of colors or some other symbology of colors coming through. Keep breathing prana in—from both directions. You are filling and supporting this new structure; allow the energy to build in preparation for the next activation.

Activation

16. Now, with a deep breath, inhale and exhale deeply, blow out the flower of life sphere to its new size. (Do this now.) Your flower of life sphere has expanded to 155 feet (47 meters) in diameter.

Figure 10.5. This eight-pointed symbol—created from two squares superimposed upon each other—was used by the Rosicrucians in the seventeenth century as a symbol for the eight points of a geometrical universe, which was guarded by eight angels

17. Allow yourself to visualize the structure known as the Gaia star, an eight-pointed star perfectly sized to reside within your flower of life sphere, supporting its new volume, structure, and size (see fig. 10.5). Visualize the space inside the flower of life sphere as crystalline teal, with the lines consisting of crystalline saffron gold, the Gaia Star. Continue your pranic breathing at this level for as long as you wish.

You have connected yourself with your new heart center at the eighth chakra. You've opened the highway to the rainbow bridge of your upper chakras, including your cosmic self. And you have connected yourself *with infinity* with*in* infinity. This now gives you access and activates—for you—your new reality. It is your energy body and connection to the *all one*.

May this meditation and activation be a blessing to you and to all you meet. May you have a day of Heaven on Earth for yourself and everyone you come in contact with.

THE VALUE OF THE VOICE ACTIVATION

The following question has been posed: "Can we do the meditation and skip the voice activation?" The answer is, you can, but the effects of the meditation don't last. If you want the activation you created with the 5D energies in your field to last for forty-eight hours you will want to complete the sound activation with it, because that anchors the 5D energies. This is your inspiration to do them together.

One student reported:

"The sonic activation matches a different part of your body with different frequencies. . . . The sound itself anchors in the visualizations that were created during the meditation. It can help you to create the universe, the cosmos, if you will. So we can experience and we can feel the cosmos within our bodies. So the feeling of not feeling well the sorrow or pain is because we did not take care of that part of the body. This is where we experience those feelings."

NEW TOOLS APPEAR

I've been accessing some very powerful tools lately while practicing this 5D MerKaBa. You can too. The latest one is the Red-Gold Energy Field. I first saw it as it appears in fig. 10.6. In less than twenty-four hours, I received the art in fig. 10.7 from my friend, artist Endre Balogh. (Both images contain red and gold coloring not shown in these black and white versions.)

It is important to note that Endre and I can go for months without touching base and then reconnect as if no time has gone by! From my perspective, his "version," although much more sophisticated than mine, is the same thing!

Figure 10.6. Red-gold energy field

Figure 10.7. Red-gold energy field by Endre Balogh

The Red-Gold Energy Field is expandable and malleable. It consists of a red outer rim whose edges are scalloped and somewhat pointy, like a holly leaf. The inside has a golden energy with more intense rays of gold emanating from the inner edges.

It came to me in this way: I was originally shown in meditation to tell a mother and her newborn twins suffering from exhaustion that she should see herself enveloped within this energy. I was told in the meditation that it would help them in every way they needed assistance. A few days later, in another healing situation, I was shown the same image and how it could be used in a specific location by enveloping any specific problem.

Having received this tool twice made me certain it was a universal one. And it was the following day when Endre sent me his most recent creation! This is what usually happens: I get an answer for a specific issue, and then the same solution appears for a different situation with a different client. Then I realize that the tool is meant for everyone.

It will allow you also to heal a situation or a physical ailment. First imagine the tool in your mind's eye. Notice that it has a jaggedness that resembles an expanding gate, it reminds me of the type of gate you put in front of stairs to limit access for children or pets. This quality of expansion is important, as it allows the image to expand to easily fit around any shape, whether it is a physical object or a part of the body that needs focused healing. The final shape can be symmetrical but does not have to be! It causes rapid healing to occur!

Because it can expand, contract, and shape shift to fit any size, you can place it, with your intention, over anything that needs extra healing of any kind! While looking at it, blink rapidly, and you'll see it start to move! It is third dimensional and fluid, so after you position it with your thought, imagine it's 5D.

11
Meet Your Dragons and the Serendipities

In addition to all the help from the Ascended Masters, Angels, and Guides I now introduce you to the dragons and serendipities, other-worldly beings who have come into the reality to assist humanity in the process of Ascension! Were dragons only mythological creatures? I doubt it, since so many artistic renderings of them from all over the world are found in our museums. They were revered and tamed. Today the dragons have returned to help humans find their true authentic selves. Even the meaning of the word points us in the direction of their true purpose, clarity. In both East and West, *dragon* comes from a root word meaning "to see clearly."

A new variety of dragons has returned to this dimension to assist and protect humans as they become fifth dimensional. Their presence at this time is vital, as they are able to shift dimensionally as well as help maintain higher vibrations of third dimension to fifth dimensions. They have returned to assist humankind with Ascension.

In 2010, dragons appeared to me in an open field while I was at a sculpture park. Storm King is a huge sculpture garden an hour north of New York City in the Hudson Valley. To be honest, I had no interest in or attachment to dragons prior to this experience. Or so I thought. It turns out I had been photographing them for quite some time, as I discovered while going through my photos! I had a vague awareness of

Figure E.1. Dragon protecting crown door

dragons since one of my sons loved dragons in his childhood fantasies, and I remember purchasing a plastic one for him once as a gift. Today dragons continue to delight and amaze me.

This time, however, the dragons were very real in my awareness. They spoke to me and urged me to understand their message! I was intrigued. Why were they here? What could they do? Answers to these questions and more came forward. First of all, dragons are not reptilian—they are warm-blooded, nurture their young, and actually keep their young's eggs warm (so I'm told). In the East they have never stopped revering dragons, and there are many stories of dragons educating humans and helping them bring order and understanding to the world.

Dragons are also part of the iconography of the spiritual beliefs of an earlier Christian era. The tapestry shown in fig. E.2 (page 208) now hangs in the Cloisters, a museum that is part of the Metropolitan Museum in New York. It was originally hanging in a Benedictine monastery—not a church, but a monastery! That says a lot. The tapestry proves that at one time dragons were revered. In a later era they were used as scapegoats and slaughtered to the point that they were moved out of this reality into another realm to recover and remain there until such time had passed that they would no longer be in danger. Why would this be? Consider the fact that dragons give clarity, and it would be hard to cover up lies with them around. They can cross over dimensional space, assisting you with your interdimensional experiences. They can help you with simple tasks like driving or moving congested traffic along. Even though they have returned, you may only see them with your inner eyes or inner awareness.

> Tail coiled, claws extended, and feet braced, this dragon is a powerful counterpart to the lion opposite. Medieval beasts, whether real or imaginary, were often imbued with symbolic meaning, as they are in animal fables today. It is not always possible, however, to reconstruct their specific intention in a given monument, and such beasts could be for "aesthetic delight," as one thirteenth-century archbishop commented. The monastery from which this fresco comes was abandoned in 1841.[1]

Figure E.2. Dragon tapestry (fresco transferred to canvas; Spanish, Castile-Leon, ca. 1200; from a room above the chapter house of the Benedictine monastery of San Pedro de Arianza, near Burgos; The Cloisters Collection, 1931: 31.38.2a, b)

WHY THEY ARE HERE

The dragons are from a life wave that has not been known to us. They carry wisdom and understanding in many esoteric categories. One area of expertise is their knowledge of the elements of earth, air, fire, and water. This means they can help you with all kinds of understanding about how to work with the elements, and all the expressions of the elements such as water undines, air sylphs, fiery salamanders, earth fairies, gnomes, and elves.*

In the history of dragons you will find two traditions: Eastern and European. As noted in the caption for figure E.2, the fresco turned to canvas art dates to about the thirteenth century. Later the European dragons were chased into oblivion by the religious persecutions of an earlier time. St. George, commonly known as the patron saint of England, was known to have slain a flesh-eating dragon to save a town in Libya. It may have been a fabrication to support the removal of dragons from worship as in far earlier works (eleventh century). St. George was depicted to have slain a human enemy as a horseman. The Eastern tradition revered dragons and held them as a source of profound wisdom. To help you understand how treasured the dragon is in Chinese culture, consider this: the dragon became the symbol that was reserved for the emperor, especially the five-clawed dragon. It is noteworthy that January 23, 2012, marked the beginning of the Chinese Year of the Dragon, the very same year as the end of the Mayan calendar. That marked the beginning of a most auspicious portal opening for all the dragons!

HOW DO YOU CALL IN YOUR DRAGONS?

I know this is beginning to sound like a fantasy—but please do not ignore your dragons' assistance. Instead, prove me wrong. Ask for your dragons to come forth, and watch for the signs that they are there. They love to be called and will show up for you, in your dreams, in the clouds, or elsewhere. Ask for their assistance. Get quiet, ask for your dragons to be present, and then ask for their names. Use what name pops into your head immediately. From that point forward call them by name. You can have more than one dragon, and they can be of either gender.

---

*Near the completion of this book, I discovered the work of Aurelia Louise Jones. My Higher Self told me there was something in volume 3 of her *Telos* series. I picked up the book and randomly opened it to the chapter on her blue dragon! I had no idea that anyone else was working with them.

Once you have a dragon's name, you may summon it and give it requests. It has adopted you as its human and is attracted to you for your specific purposes. *Never give the names of your dragons to anyone unless you totally trust that person to respect and honor the names.* When your dragons generously share their names with you, it is akin to offering their services, because now you may invite them in by name, seeking their help! And they do love it when you need them and call to them for help!

A chiropractor friend of mine who was going through some tough times endlessly complained to me about his situation. I asked him to close his eyes and ask to see his dragon and to request the name of his dragon. I stepped away for a few moments. When I returned, he was crying tears of gratitude! His dragon was iridescent white and gave him her name.

You can add the dragons to your collection of tools to help you navigate the very challenging world in front of you. You can ask your dragons to search out and bring to you helpers or resources to assist your projects. Even more importantly, the dragons can help you recognize the truth as it is spoken to you. In fig. E.3 is a dragon incense burner, which I've lovingly nicknamed my "smoking Dragon."

The dragons are both symbolic and real when they appear in a dream. They are fourth-dimensional elementals with their own intelligence and programs of service. They are more independent than earth elementals like gnomes, fairies, and elves. They have returned to the Earth at this time to help humanity. Their purpose is related to communications, travel, and finding both your physical and metaphysical way.

Optimizing Your Dragons

Why do we need their help? With all the changes in our lives—Earth changes, spiritual changes, work, society, and so on—there can be false starts, misdirection, and uncertainty. The dragons are back to help us see clearly! You don't need dragons to do this for you, of course, if you

Figure E.3. Dragon incense burner

have an activated MerKaBa and a solid Higher Self connection. But who couldn't use a little extra help? Many of us, even with these skills, have come to rely on the dragons for miracles, wisdom, and clarity of every kind. You can too.

You can ask them to "take over the driving" or help you see and understand what you haven't seen or what you need to see. You can ask them to help you get where you are going. I always ask for help for the oncoming traffic as well as the traffic going my way. Why not? I'm calling in their help, and they love to do it!

Recently, my husband and I were driving down a very busy Seattle street, and I could see wall-to-wall cars in busy traffic everywhere. We could see that the interstate below us as well as the road we were on were both jammed with cars. I looked at my husband, who was driving, and said, "We need to call the dragons!" So much heavy traffic everywhere! So I called on our dragons by name. We asked for them to help us and help everyone around us so that everyone would get where they needed to go with grace and ease. Within a few minutes, my husband spontaneously commented, "I have never seen or driven through all these green traffic lights straight away with no obstacles." (This was for at least twenty lights!) And all the lights ahead of us were still green as well! As he said this, I said to myself and then out loud to him, "It must be the dragons!"

I'm also getting more and more feedback from clients who are thanking me for alerting them to the dragons' help. One woman called me to tell me her dragons made it possible for her to make it to class on time—in record time. Another friend coming to see me was traveling on the "most difficult highway in the USA" according to truckers (the Cross Bronx Expressway). He made it in record time and also found parking right in front of my building in New York—not always easy!

In another example a customer had a dream before she knew me that was actually trying to "wake her up" to the dragons' help. She originally was feeling very sorry for herself. Without knowing why, in our brief exchange, I suggested she work with her dragons. Here is her response:

"It is interesting you mentioned dragons. A few months ago I had a dream. I was in a very colorful, magical place where there were many dragons of many different colors. I was standing in the valley where two dragons came to meet me, one black and one white. I was standing in the middle of the two, reaching my hands out to each of them. People that were nearby were whispering that these dragons had never let anyone touch them before. I woke up soon after that."

My interpretation of her dream is that she needs to equally embrace the light and the dark. This is a message we can all use. So dear heart, know that you can, you must, call on your dragons to harness incredible power tailored just for you. They are back because the need for human discernment is greater than ever.

Another example comes from my friends Kelly and Doug, who live in New England. He has an arduous commute to and from work with tons of traffic, cars pulling into traffic, narrow New England roads with curves, and general rush hour craziness. Although he loves his job, he doesn't like the commute at all. It takes a huge amount of effort and energy for him to navigate through this intense driving maze daily.

One day, he decided to "take my word for it" and invite the dragons to work with him to take over the driving to and from work. To his utter amazement, no one pulled out in front of him or cut him off, no one "almost" hit him, and other drivers "made way" for him. He announced to his wife that evening that he would be asking the dragons for help every day!

Then there was the recent time when my husband and I were in England for a week driving all over the countryside in a rental car. He likes to navigate, and I like to drive. UK driving is always challenging for those of us used to driving on the other side of the road. At first, like most drivers, I had a bit of trouble staying close enough to the center. However, when I asked the dragons to take over the driving—we not only drove well but were one day "shown" a great restaurant that we could go to for dinner later that evening when we "missed our turnoff." We would never have seen or found this incredible restaurant without that extra dragon direction detection. In addition, I actually felt my brain working differently while driving on the left side of the road. Maybe that's the way our brain is supposed to work. I can attest to the help they gave us, because I couldn't imagine doing that without the extra help of the archangels and the dragons!

Don't take my word for it. Give it a try. Your dragons will help you unlock the secrets of dimensional living at every level. You must be ready for the next step, and they will help you find your way. I now think that it may have been the dragons who gave me the title, *Waking Up in 5D*!

Fear of Flying

My friend and fabulous craniosacral healer, Carol Kakoczky, had been listening to me explaining about the dragons week after week in my healing sessions with her. It finally sank in. Last week she told me about the trip she and her husband undertook. She's always been afraid to fly. As her plane was preparing to take off, she became overcome with her fear of being airborne and decided to call in "her" dragons.

She was shocked and amazed that her dragons showed up! Doing craniosacral work has activated her inner vision, her third eye, developing her natural talent. Being able to see with her inner eye at this moment was indeed profound! Not only could she see the dragons, there were three of them! There was a green one on the left wing, a red one on the right wing, and a white one on the top of the fuselage! Their appearance definitely calmed her. During the flight, when the air got a bit bumpy and she found herself overreacting with the panicked thought, "I'm gonna die," the white dragon spoke to her and said, "Do you want to live?" Of course "Yes" was her immediate reply. Instantly she felt completely relaxed! She's still talking about that experience.

Your turn. Give it a try. Ask your dragons to appear to you in your next meditation. Write me your experiences! I want to know. Even the children are pulling them in. Witness the sidewalk drawing (see fig. E.4) I discovered last week at a local park.

My clearing team has seen large black dragons—that we now think

Figure E.4. Dragon drawing on sidewalk

were holding back the usurping of power! So when you encounter the abuses of power, you can call in dragons to help hold those back! This alone would be a sufficient reason for the large number of the dragons supporting humanity now!

Dragon Energy

The dragon is considered the mightiest and most auspicious of the twelve animals of the Chinese zodiac. The dragon's number *five* is the luckiest of all the sacred numbers; it fits that the dragon is the fifth animal of the series. People born in the dragon years are said to be creative, expansive, strong, and lucky. Naturally the babies born in a dragon year are believed to be the most favored, likely to enjoy long life, prosperity, good health, and smooth birth and to have happy offspring, friendship, and honor—all the blessings of a life lived well in accord with the will of heaven *and* the respect of men.

Figure E.5. Dragon ironwork

In *Transition to the Golden Age in 2032,* Diana Cooper writes about the dragons. Even though she wrote this excerpt about the country of Japan, I believe it applies to humanity everywhere.

> Japan has very strong connections with dragon energy. Dragons are fourth dimensional elementals that can help us tremendously when we are open to them. Dragons bring strength, protection and companionship to support communities as outmoded structures break down. This will help them to rise above their problems and open up to higher spiritual dimensions.[2]

The fire dragon uses the color of bright red, which goes very well with the Imperial yellow silk and gold. To the Chinese the dragon represents unlimited potential and unlimited possibilities. This is why in the Chinese tradition you might hear someone speaking of a newborn son by referring to him as a "dragon."

The dragon is also known as a shape shifter, able to change from the size of a small worm to being as big as the sky. This is why we see so many dragon shapes in the clouds, because the clouds or the sylphs are replicating or showing us what is already there in reality. Many of us see our dragons in iridescent rainbows. They can hide within the clouds and lakes and rivers and then can also turn into water.

No matter what elements your dragon may call home, it has validity, mutability, and the all-embracing qualities of water. All dragons are yang but carry the full potential of being yin—in various expressions (like the water dragon pictured in fig. E.6—water dragons also have a serpent quality to their form).

Figure E.6. Kyoto water dragon located on the ascent to Mt. Kurama in Kyoto, Japan—the dragon actually disperses the water like a faucet for the cleansing ceremony that pilgrims make before their ascent to this sacred mountain, deemed to be the location that Sanat Kumara landed his spaceship

THE SERENDIPITIES

Remember the sad story of my sister's untimely death? Not only did our two brothers share her car accident experience, my brother's oldest son—who worked for a French electrical company as an engineer and is fluent in French—just happened to be on his way to O'Hare to go to Paris (where my sister and her family lived) when they got the news of my sister's disaster, What a relief to have the only French-speaking family member on his way to Paris before any others of us could get on a plane!

Have you noticed your own synchronicities and serendipities occurring more often? This is a way to realize you are being graced with a new being—the Serendipities, *not* serendipity! The new 5D MerKaBa helps you open your higher chakras. As your tenth chakra opens, the Serendipities are more common. This is because you've allowed the energy of higher consciousness to "match" you with significant opportunities. And as a wonderful serendipity addition, the presence of the Serendipities helps you open your higher chakras! It works both ways: call them in, and your tenth chakra opens easier. As you welcome the Serendipities, you make it easier to hold higher energy coming in through your tenth chakra. Remember, everything you do assists humanity with the full Ascension of the planet.

Here's an example: I was in the car with my husband, near our Seattle home. Our iPod was automatically scrolling through various songs from his vast music library when singer Brandi Carlile came up. I had never heard her sing. As I listened to her, I commented to my husband, "I really like her music. We should go see her sometime." I spoke this as if I knew that we could see her locally; I didn't know why I said that. My husband nodded and said, "Well, she's from the Seattle area, you know, and she sometimes performs with the Seattle Symphony." He added, "I'll go online and see." The next day he informed me that he was holding tickets for the Sunday after Thanksgiving, when she was indeed performing with the Seattle Symphony!

I was totally amazed that tickets had become available just a few days earlier, about six weeks before the concert! My husband had plenty of time to get great seats, even though it sold out in a few days. We had a wonderful time. My husband's music collection is large and varied—songs come up randomly on our iPod. I was happily "flowing in 5D" when I responded to my enjoyment of her music with the suggestion that we go see her. Even I didn't know I was going to say that! I'm continually delighted at what flows through me this way, in terms of getting what we want and enjoying our lives. Thank you, Serendipities.

Here's another very recent instance. At dinner yesterday my husband told me that while I was going to be in New York, he had gained yet another Philadelphia client who called him and wanted him in Philly next week. This meant he now had two appointments back-to-back on one trip to the Philadelphia area. He said, "In true Maureen fashion I've managed to acquire two completely unrelated clients in the same city at the same time!" Ladies and gentlemen—*this* is what it's like to live in 5D. Magic happens all the time. These happy coincidences are your new normal. Welcome to a most magical integration into the fifth dimension. This is just the beginning!

Terri and the Serendipities

When one of the Akashic Records guides, Terri Young, called me one morning recently to tell me of her experiences with the Serendipities, I wasn't surprised! I was delighted. They introduced themselves directly to her. She is hoping to write a book about her experiences someday. In a personal correspondence to me she wrote:

As I was waking up, I heard, "We are the Serendipities," *not* "a serendipity." After taking a huge breath, I said to those that were speaking to me, "HUH??"

Let me begin by saying that I love talking about a serendipitous happening, and I love seeing all the steps that it—that wonderful experience—took to get me there. So having a conversation with the Serendipities was a whole new place to be.

I also want to add that I love the angels. We have conversations often, especially if I have a problem. We communicate quite frequently in the dreamtime right before sleep and in the wake-time as I am awaking. I ask Archangel Michael and his 100% God-light retinue to be with me when I am making decisions and when I am having a hard time just living in this dense world.

So having the Serendipities announce themselves as these *beings*— well, their explanation of themselves was very surprising. Once I was awake enough to respond, I asked, "Why me?" But the answer I got was to actually see them. They bounced. . . . A little like small bubbles of champagne. I felt their presence and was so happy and light that all I could do was smile. They promptly responded with more of their bubbliness and were extremely happy to let me know that they also loved it when I noticed that they had worked their magic to move things in order for—get ready for it—*miracles*!

Serendipities are the movers and shakers of miracles. Haven't we all experienced having something work out and we were honestly not sure exactly how *it all worked out,* but it did? Well they want us to know of their existence and want us to know that they are so happy to work for us. All we have to do is ask.

So, here is how it works. Have you ever said to yourself, "I have to remember—(fill in the blank)"? And then you find yourself opening a cupboard or a door, and then you remember what it was you needed? These small steps lead you to get what you wanted. Thank the Serendipities. There's so much fun to be had with them! Life can get easier and easier if you will just let them in.

Say, "Serendipities, help me to get all that needs to be done in an easier and simpler way today." Then disconnect from what you expect. Let them do their magic. I guarantee that life will get so sweet. You can also ask for love beams from the Serendipities. The love beam is a sweet download. It starts with a loving spaciousness in your heart. You feel this love move through your body within and between all spaces. Your vibration of love becomes a column of light from the eleventh chakra down your pranic tube to Mother Earth. As you feel this loving vibration, you know that you can softly use this to scan your own body.

"Finally," they offered, "we are also beings of light that can push time into a slower or faster speed. We are also able to help with thoughts that do not serve you. If you are open, then you can change your mind about something that is not working for you. Change your mind and it will change your experience. We are also able to hear your worries and we are able to help with these in small, minor ways that make your path smoother."

The Serendipities are with you. "Give us a chance to help," they say, "and we can make miracles."

With delight, Terri Young

Thank you, Terri, for being an incredible messenger of love and light!

12
What's Next?

Much is happening on this planet, in this planet, and to this planet. First of all, the liberation has already occurred. We are now in the implementation phase, which takes a long time. As we are in a free will zone, nothing happens that we haven't orchestrated at some level. The "game" here is almost over, and we have many blessings that are readily available.

The most important action for you is to recognize who you are, and that as a being carrying a spark of the Divine, you have a right to demand that all of the forces of heaven support you, and every aspect of your life. Remember that when you face some obstacle that appears real. Demand that it be cleared and removed. Meditate regularly, and relax—the hard part is over.

Are you in? It's up to you! Many beings of *light* are working with you, and there are latent energies that emerge to assist you when you *decide* to accept all improvements, all available upgrades, so you change your matrix. It's time to decide you will do your part, because it cannot and will not happen without you. Most of what you will do is intention work. This is *very powerful* intention work. This is *not* the run of the mill feel-good type of work. Because we are in a planetary transformation we are being given the opportunity to restructure our cellular and molecular framework right down to our DNA and RNA.

MOVING BEYOND POLARITY

We're moving out of the game of polarity into a new game. In 2002 I unexpectedly came upon the mosaic of Archangel Michael with his sword doing a battle somersault. It was on the wall of the Paris Metro station beneath Notre Dame. As I stood in front of this amazing, beautiful art, Archangel Michael delivered a message directly to me. He said that humanity only needs a homeopathic dose of negativity to hold the balance of light.

How many times have we heard teachers say, "Well, if there's more light, then there is more darkness"? Every time I would hear this I would always hold back and not understand. In my own thinking I could not comprehend that we would allow any more darkness in this world. When you realize the game is changing, you can see why this new information (very little darkness required) would make more sense, because it would make the transition from polarity much easier. In homeopathy, the energetic signature of an herb in the final preparation is so minute that it does not appear to be present in a chemical analysis. I believe Archangel Michael gave me this message so that we could understand that it is no longer true that having more light on this planet means more darkness. I also believe it is so that we will understand that as long as we have polarity there will be some darkness, but it might be so minuscule that it is not discernable to us.

Imagine that there is so much light here that all the evil that we know about *is* the homeopathic dose. Instantly we have increased the light on the planet because we have now put all of our attention on the light instead of the stuff we don't want. For example, if we ask, "What about all the bad people in the world?" Who are we talking about? The murderers, the thieves, whomever. Information came through me in response to this question, and I was in awe about what channeled through. Let's start by calling bad guys "the alligators." Every time you think about them you are feeding them.

You can understand this concept of feeding them by calling to mind something you have probably noticed in a situation when you are talking to a friend you are with about someone else in the same room, and the person you have been discussing looks up and smiles at you or comes over. And you think to yourself, "Did he know we were talking about him?" And the answer is, energetically, "Yes." I have always been very sensitive. As a child, my older brother teased me. One time when I began to wail, my mother turned to my brother and said, "Stop what you're doing." He protested, saying, "All I did was look at her." And my mother responded, "Well then, don't look at her." And I say to you, don't look at the darkness and you won't feed alligators.

When you think about or judge the behavior of the bad guys we have renamed alligators, you give them more energy with your emotion. The only way to avoid feeding them is to decide that they will have their own battle and it doesn't involve you. When you force yourself to examine the concept of no more karma, you can no longer have judgments about the thieves and the murderers. The alligators have used force to take over to some degree. But this force they have used will not be used to stop them. Instead, they will be consumed by love. Source will love them anyway. Perfect love casts out darkness. All-encompassing love consumes it.

When you do the 5D MerKaBa, you bring in so much light that they get drowned out. Our job is to keep our eye on the light, and to do our best to stay out of judgment of the darkness that is still here. You and I cannot do anything about that darkness. We can do something about the light quotient. That's what we are good at. There are people who deal with the alligators; that's their job. And we must do ours.

WHAT CAN YOU DO?

Consider the twelve recognitions that will guide you to the new you, the new reality, and give you the basis for the new game in town.

1. Recognize that your Higher Self is *you,* and how to access it.
2. Recognize that your Higher Self can guide you.
3. Recognize the benefit of asking your Higher Self about everything.
4. Recognize that a blow to the heart is rocket fuel for your Ascension.
5. Recognize that you are the co-creator of your reality.
6. Recognize that you can change this reality at will.
7. Recognize that the way you receive is unrelated to the giver.
8. Recognize that all individuals are on their own journey.
9. Recognize that you are the center of your universe.
10. Recognize each day you have a clean slate (no more karma).
11. Recognize that you have an obligation to act with integrity.
12. Be willing to stay connected to your Higher Self.

Use the Higher Self Connection to Gain Knowledge

We use our egos to learn and familiarize ourselves with the world around us. At maturity, the ego is no longer needed but has become so powerful that we continue to rely on it instead of growing our Higher Self awareness. This gives the term "growing up" much greater meaning! It's time to grow up. The obvious conclusion of waking up your Higher Self connection is that your ego and Higher Self can become one will, your God will.

Use the Higher Self to Co-Create with God

Within the mind of God is all perfection and all-knowingness. Yet this mind does not contain all the experiences that have yet to be experienced. This is a common misnomer, because even the Akashic Records hold probable futures and do not hold all possible futures until there is energy supporting a specific direction.

From the Akashic Records

So we say to you from on high: allow yourself to be open and receptive to the Divine Self—that hidden inner wisdom that represents the version of you that is fully plugged into God to be present and in your consciousness. We will do this with you.

We ask that you find a quiet place, right now, and invite you to go on a meditation journey with us. As you relax in this moment, ask your Higher Self to join you in your heart. Your Higher Self is fully plugged into God, and when that part of you merges with your heart, you now have access to the mind of God.

From this point, ask for the mind of God to overshadow you, to inspire you, to evolve you. Ask for the mind of God to step in and fill your mind with this deep love that God holds for you. This love will permeate everything about you. It will enable you to then let your mind relax, let your ego relax, and let the mind of God move through you, through your heart to create your divine expression.

This is one way to merge your ego with your Divine Self.

Change Reality with Your Bedtime Story

For starters, you can create a bedtime matrix. Mine looks like this:

I ask that I be escorted to an etheric retreat that is ideally suited for me. I ask that I might be granted permission to attend the Ascension retreat of Serapis Bey.* I ask that my physical body be taken to a rejuvenation chamber or a healing chamber, whichever my Higher Self and guides recommend for me this night. I also claim an energetic Faraday cage around my bed, to insulate me from all harmful energies of any kind. I ask that I awaken well rested and refreshed, regardless of what the night may hold.

I actually have this on a small piece of paper with a photo of a bed to remind me to use it when I crawl in bed. I rarely read it, but the picture reminds me to make the invocation.

---

*Serapis Bey, also known as Ancient of Days, represents source code from mathematics and God determination.

Change Reality with Your Conversation about Family and Friends

Learn to "change your story" about others. For example, one of my clients shared with me her fear of her sister. Her wealthy sister, a Sikh, was coming for a visit. She always felt uncomfortable in her presence, and she always felt small and insignificant while with her. She wanted the kind of good, close relationship that sisters can have. I then suggested she change her story. She would envision herself doing the happy dance after their visit, sharing with friends how much fun they had, and telling others how happy she was to have built an amazing connection with her sister. In this client's case, she called me after her sister's visit and reported what a wonderful time she had with her and how they had reconnected in a whole new way! She was doing the happy dance, just as she had envisioned.

Depending on your particular situation, you might start with something like, "My brother, Tom, is ready to talk to Mom again." Or, "My brother, Dana, and his wife, are ready to take Mom into their home." Like a movie of the mind, you see the outcome that pleases you, and you include a real-time conversation that anchors it into your current reality. This ensures the outcome, and of course you are also using your joy and love to see how happy this outcome makes you!

Change Reality with Your Conversation about Others

One way to do this is to stop engaging in political debate. Political gossip can be so damaging because it gives energy to the negative. No matter what the situation is, whether you are thinking about a famous person or the president of any country, change your story! Decide to create a *new* pathway for them to follow. The way you do this is to create new stories about them, so you don't energetically hold them in their patterns (real or imagined).

You can do this with anyone. If you decide to do this, every time you think of the specific person, you would think a new and simple story about her. Simple is best for this approach. For example, you might think to yourself, "I'm focusing on the president of (any country) who is truly representing the will of the people and serves no single master! She is a channel for wisdom in action in government."

This works amazingly well. You don't do or say anything to the person at the center of your thoughts. You just change your story about her whenever you think of her. Your energy is a powerful tool that can be used to help yourself and others to take the highest road possible. That new version of reality gets more and more real as you repeat it in your head in response to anything negative or dark. That is the true beauty of it. Of course you can't make others' choices, but it gives them energetic permission to have a new story. It's amazing how others pick up our sweet expectations of them, sent lovingly and with compassion, and usually they meet them. Very often people will change their patterns shortly after they have been given energetic permission to do so. I have found this to be an exceptional, powerful tool.

Many years ago I had a bathroom in my house, just off the family room. It was often cold and had a little bit of mold in the corners above the shower. I never liked that bathroom. When it had a flood and holes were made in the wall to repair the pipes, I decided to change the energy. After removing the wallpaper, I wrote cute little sayings on the walls like, "This is such a cute bathroom. This bathroom is in just the right space. This bathroom has sweet energy." Then we put new wallpaper up, completely covering the words. Imagine my amused surprise when houseguests using the bathroom would come back into the kitchen reciting what I had written underneath the wallpaper!

✳ RESPONDING TO WORLDWIDE DIFFICULTIES

I have been getting visuals on how to use the 5D MerKaBa Meditation actively for all humanity, to heal situations (such as wildfires, hurricane, flood, earthquake, and so on) on the planet. This is especially powerful if you are in the middle of a troubling situation or know of someone who is experiencing one.

1. Imagine you have just finished the 5D Multidimensional MerKaBa.
2. Next, think of the situation, and send a taproot from your pranic tube deep into the earth.
3. Connect with the elements of earth, air, fire, and water. Tune to the energies, and become one with them.
4. Ask the element involved to calm down and stabilize. Love it, thank it, and cherish it, surrounding it with love. See ease. Feel ease.

We have the energy of the cosmos coming through us, which gives direct God-Source solution energy that we direct into our actions such as this.

ENCOURAGING MESSAGES OF LIGHT

These questions in the Akashic Field were answered directly by the Goddess of Liberty and the Lords of Light, channeled through Maureen.

Will There Be Another War?

No. The military machine is rapidly being dismantled. Many schools and other networks are in place to deal with the rapid release of military trained individuals. The most difficult part is giving their service a value and a place in history.

Forces of light above and beyond are looking at all scenarios and none include a war. Certain memories of possibilities have been cleared from reality. From a practical sense, the biggest secret on the planet known to those with access to the military machine is that the nuclear weapons have been immobilized and many systems shut down or rendered inoperable. Those whose agenda is war have been warned, and they are simply posturing. Know that their day has expired.*

---

*A well documented incident on Malmstrom AFB in 1967 illustrates this point. www.cufon.org/cufon/malmstrom/malm1.htm.

Goddess of Liberty Continues

There will not be a nuclear war. There will not be a World War III. This is not possible, as humanity has passed the point of no return and has moved past that potentiality. Just like a miscarriage may occur only early in a pregnancy, you are now past that risk factor. This is because the electronic capabilities of the nuclear warhead have been disengaged and destroyed. It is no longer possible for the military machine to ignite a world war.

This Is Lord Sanat Kumara

Learning this [5D MerKaBa] meditation is a sacred opportunity for you. Your practicing it will turn the tide for the planet. It will change your life as well. You will experience greater love, opportunity, joy, connections; in short, life will be easier, and you need not take my word for it. If you forget to do it for a day or two, you will wonder what is wrong. And we ask you to remember this moment, where you were told you will find out soon enough. There will be more information later. Let it suffice for now that you are remarkable human beings to have chosen this work at this time. We commend you for your service. And we ask that if you falter you call upon us to assist you, as we are never far from you. Your devotion is like a lighthouse and will attract us, on the other side, and it will also attract others who wish to know and understand more. That is all.

This Is the Great Divine Director

I join you this day to reinforce your own connection with your Divine Self. You may call to me to expand beyond your capabilities at this time. The tide has turned on planet Earth. So there is nothing to fear. Keep your dates with destiny. Do not change your plans just because you have been reassured or know something. Instead stay in your heart. Let yourself be influenced by your Higher Self. Pray for others.

You might offer, "I pray this for myself and for all of humanity" at the end of any prayer. Pray for those you love, and pray for those you don't. Pray to love those that you don't, and you will fall in love with those you do not love now. And you will no longer feel the need to not love them. When you feel weak and afraid that you will not obtain your goal, call to me and I will infuse you with my great blue energy of will and divine direction. I am the Great Divine Director.

YOU CAN MAKE A DIFFERENCE!

It is useful to remember that it doesn't take much in the way of making change. You can make a difference. Do this by forming into groups. Whether in your yoga center, bookstore, coffee shop, or living room, gather in small groups to have discussions. Maybe you will follow a storyline and create a study group. Maybe you will achieve something that will allow you to co-create in the universe.

There are new grids being created every day to support you. Many new grids that are purposefully left blank or empty for your creations have been put in place. Everything, and I mean everything, is up for renegotiation and for reevaluation. However, it is totally up to you what happens next. You are on the road to Ascension. How long it takes and what mode of transportation you use is your choice!

Although some would tell you everything that has ever been created already exists, if that were true, you wouldn't need to be a co-creator with God! In fact, we are constantly creating something new, wonderful, and powerful. Recognize that this is part of our prime directive; go ahead and add to the database!

Notes

2. HOW WE PROCESS INFORMATION

1. Jonah Lehrer, *How We Decide* (New York: Houghton Mifflin Harcourt, 2009).
2. Roy F. Baumeister, "Conquer Yourself, Conquer the World," *Scientific American,* April 2015.

5. YOUR EMOTIONS CARRY THE KEY

1. Mark L. Prophet and Elizabeth Clare Prophet, *The Masters and Their Retreats* (Corwin Springs, MT: Summit University Press, 2003) 158.

6. LANGUAGE OF FIFTH DIMENSION

1. Josh Richardson, "How to Prevent Limitation and Proceed to Your Power," PreventDisease.com, March 20, 2014, http://preventdisease.com/news/14/032014_Prevent-Limitation-Proceed-To-Your-Power.shtml.

7. THE TIME AND SPACE CONTINUUM

1. "Introduction to GCP," The Global Consciousness Project, http://noosphere.princeton.edu/gcpintro.html.
2. James Twyman, "World Synchronized Meditation Miracle," https://jt208.infusionsoft.com/app/hostedEmail/15749367/7321f8c6578bef6a?inf_contact_key=d33eb85e0a2f4f05e99b65a6aec03b8ad091c07d14d14bef26217da7aa9898e6.

10. BECOMING FIFTH DIMENSIONAL AND ACTIVATING THE HIGHER CHAKRAS

1. Joseph Mercola, "How Sun Exposure Improves Your Immune Function," Mercola, January 23, 2017, http://articles.mercola.com/sites/articles /archive/2017/01/23/how-sun-exposure-improves-immune-function.aspx.

2. Richard Weller, "Could the Sun Be Good for Your Heart?," TED, www .ted.com/talks/richard_weller_could_the_sun_be_good_for_your_heart.

3. Andrew Knoll, "N.H.L. Teams Dream of a Title After a Good Night's Sleep," *New York Times*, April 24, 2016, www.nytimes.com/2016/04/25 /sports/hockey/nhl-playoffs-sleep.html?_r=0.

4. Tom Kenyon, "White Gold Alchemy," Tom Kenyon.com, http:// tomkenyon.com/store/white-gold-alchemy.

5. Christina Congleton, Britta K. Hölzel, and Sara W. Lazar, "Mindfulness Can Literally Change Your Brain," Harvard Business Review, January 8, 2015, https://hbr.org/2015/01/mindfulness-can-literally-change-your-brain.

6. Endre Balogh, "Sacred Geometries—Art," Endre Fine Photographic Art, http://endre-balogh.pixels.com/collections/sacred+geometries.

11. MEET YOUR DRAGONS AND THE SERENDIPITIES

1. "Dragon," The MET, www.metmuseum.org/art/collection/search/471062.

2. Diana Cooper, *Transition to the Golden Age in 2032* (Findhorn, Scotland: Findhorn Press, 2011).

Suggested Resources

The primary source for the resources mentioned in this book and the other resources I offer is my website, **www.maureenstgermain.com**. There you will find links to all of my books, CDs, MP3s, essential oils, events, and classes. Below are listed some of the specific resources recommended in this book and the free downloads of meditations being offered along with it.

FREE MEDITATIONS

The following meditations are available for download from **www.MaureenStGermain.com/5DBonus.**

Crystal Elohim Meditation

I highly recommend you use this empowering energetic tool. It will greatly expand your abilities, your consciousness, and your fifth-dimensional expression. The Elohim channeled this CD in 1994. At the time, they insisted that I drop everything and create the guided meditation. It is a powerful tool. Humanity is evolving to a crystal-line structure, this we know. Some of this may be difficult, strange, or painful. Knowing this, avail yourself of this wonderful opportunity to connect with the energy of the Crystal Elohim to assist you through this process of transformation. By choosing to do this work, you accept the opportunity that is being offered. Remember also that this work is cyclical, in that your efforts with the Crystal Elohim connect you to the crystal grids and the Christ consciousness grid and vice versa. The Christ consciousness grid will assist you in bringing forth your most evolved self, into your physical existence, your fifth-dimensional self.

Wheel Within the Wheel Angel Meditation

This remarkable, transformative meditation was named after the ancient name for the MerKaBa—Wheel Within the Wheel. This meditation will invite the cosmic energies that are now available to move you into a new space. It will help you activate your DNA changes and speed up your evolution. These cosmic energies are changing who you are and allow you to shift to higher frequencies. Beautiful background music written by me is included in this meditation.

Make Your Year a Good One! Guided Meditation

This amazing meditation takes you through a series of affirmations to set the stage for a prosperous, productive year and life. It was created for a specific client dealing with depression, who was unable to even name what she wanted. All she could do is name what she didn't want! I transformed each of her fears to their highest outcome, which became the affirmations. Beautiful background music written by me is included in this meditation.

Divine Government Meditation

The six-minute prayer actually demands our sovereignty and claims divine intervention. It's one tool I recommend you use daily.

Triple Mantra Meditation

The Triple Mantra was channeled directly from the Akashic Records to assist a client in manifesting a more evolved version of himself. After the session, I was directed to make a guided meditation of the triple mantra for use by anyone. This eight-minute guided meditation could be used for rejuvenation or healing behaviors, attitudes, or anything you wish were different about you! It allows one to identify a key area of improvement and follow the instructions, allowing a more evolved you to appear before you and to merge with. Users have reported that it is a remarkable tool to bring in a level of mastery they had not been able to achieve any other way.

OTHER USEFUL RESOURCES FOR PURCHASE

Mantras for Ascension

The CD and the MP3 include the Hathor Chant (track 1) and the Kadoish Chant (track 2).

Flower of Life MerKaBa Classic DVD

This is a wonderful recording of the original 17-Breath MerKaBa Meditation. In this three-hour-plus MerKaBa classic training video, I guide you through the seventeen steps of the original meditation.

Multi-Dimensional 5D MerKaBa Meditation

This meditation will open you up to your fifth-dimensional self in a new and powerful way. It will enable you to activate your 8th, 9th, 10th, 11th, and 12th chakras. This new meditation almost always improves all your meditations, your contentment, and your flow of cosmic energy and releases the newer DNA frequencies to be reproduced in the body. Once you start to practice this new meditation—you will desire to continue it because it is so powerful, creating substantial changes by expanding who you really are!

The Fountain of Youth Guided Meditation

The Fountain of Youth guided meditation will literally make you younger. It is a very powerful tool that you can purchase, along with the AroMandalas essential oil blend "Fountain of Youth." Together, they will clear you of irritation and resentment and fill you with acceptance and allowing. They will aid the adaptation of your body to the new incoming photon belt energies and clear you of that which holds you back.

Beyond the Flower of Life, *by Maureen J. St. Germain*

Multidimensional Activation of your Higher Self, the Inner Guru; Advanced MerKaBa Teachings, Sacred Geometry and the Opening of your Heart. If you are looking to enhance your meditation practice or are ready to take it to the next level, this book was written with you in mind. Published by Phoenix Rising Publishing, a division of Transformational Enterprises, Inc., New York.

Reweaving the Fabric of Your Reality: Self-Study Guide for Personal Transformation, *by Maureen J. St. Germain*

This is the long-awaited, newly revised book on entities as taught by the Ascended Masters through me. Understand and practice ceremonies and invocations to achieve and maintain clarity. Reweaving helps you understand and clear entities, clear curses, clear the suicide entity, and much, much more. This book is all about giving yourself a makeover of love and light.

AroMandalas®

AroMandalas are essential oil blends channeled by Mary Magdalene to clear major emotional wounds of being human and to elevate human consciousness to its Divine Self. These blends heal and repair emotional wounds; the table below shows the aspects of healing and higher consciousness that are created when the wounds are cleared with AroMandalas.

These blends also serve to open the hologram around the three-dimensional experience by magnetizing and allowing access to higher dimensions as each emotional wound is cleared and replaced with an abundance of the antithesis. They can be purchased on my website, www.maureenstgermain.com. The table on the following pages describes how these blends might be used for emotional wounds as well as for healing and higher consciousness.

The Sacred Rings

The Sacred Rings, a Sacrament of the Nemenhah Native American Church, provide a method to help balance our elemental energies, through the application of Bliss Oils to the five energetic acupuncture circuits discovered by C. Norman Shealy, M.D., Ph.D. They can be found at https://normshealy.com/the-sacred-rings.

AROMANDALAS FOR
EMOTIONAL WOUNDS AND HEALING

AroMandalas Blend	Replacing Human-Emotional Wound	With Healing and Higher Consciousness
Angel Guidance	Helpless	Empowerment—power lies within and angels stand ready to assist
Crystal Elohim	Not belonging	All is One—restores original blueprint and DNA
Fountain of Youth	Resentment/frustration	Acceptance—helps cellular memory clear mass consciousness miasmas to reflect eternal youth
MerKaBa Mystique	Anger/rage	Compassion—at peace with self and the world
Pyramid Echoes	Disappointment	Nonjudgment—releases old habits and useless expressions of four lower bodies
River Dancing	Desperation	Abundance—awakens expressions of fulfillment and plenty
Passages (Volumes I, II, or III)	Loss	Letting go—clears narrow and limiting belief system and paves the way for your Journey of Power in this lifetime
Mantra	Feeling trapped	Freedom—moving on to higher levels of experience
Magdalene Trilogy	Being martyr/victim	Awakens, unifies, and completes the balance of Divine Male and Divine Female in service to humanity
Bethany	Being martyr/male or female	My life is service (not servitude)
The Way	Victim/male	To self/others—one must first recognize his own healing before truly serving others
The Wisdom	Victim/female	To self/others—one must first recognize her own healing before truly serving others
Dolphin Dreams	Despair	Restores joy and playfulness

AroMandalas Blend	Replacing Human-Emotional Wound	With Healing and Higher Consciousness
Himalayan High	Terror	Courage—daring to dream
Andean Alchemy	Heartsickness	Heart chakra opens to higher expression of love
OCTA	Shame	Self-worth/self-acceptance; healing karmic shame for self, family, and planet
Akasha	Longing	Ascension to Higher Realms—understanding what it means to be human on an animate planet and participate in a shift in consciousness
Genie in a Bottle	Feeling overwhelmed	New possibilities—breaking free of thought forms that control my life
Reweaving	Feeling violated	Expression of original intent—every experience will benefit life's journey
Kyphi—Sacred to Isis	See below	Creating a time machine in a bottle
Sacred Journey	See below	Recognizing the sacredness of being human
Inner Guru	Ascension blends—seed energy	Awakens your Inner Guru and explores the dimensions beyond the reality of your current experience; helps with your meditation experience to discover a more heart-centered awareness
Covenant	Ascension Blends—seed energy	Helps to strengthen the bond between your soul and earthly body
Convergence	Ascension blends—Seed energy	This unique combination of oils touches the deep secrets of the soul and reminds us that we are not alone in the universe. It brings forth the spiritual awareness needed to move forward with courage and fortitude

Index